SPRING
PROCESSIONAL

ENCOUNTERS WITH A WAKING WORLD

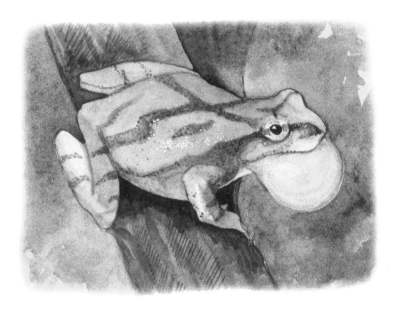

CRAIG NEWBERGER

ILLUSTRATIONS BY SHERRIE YORK

PHOTOGRAPHS BY STEVE MORELLO
UNLESS OTHERWISE NOTED

APPENDIX BY RON SMITH

Grackle Publishing - Ambler, Pennsylvania

Grackle
An imprint of Grackle Publishing, LLC
gracklepublishing.com

Library of Congress Control Number: 2022932935
ISBN: 978-1-951620-11-0 (pbk.)
ISBN: 978-1-951620-12-7 (ebook)

To Trudy
with infinite love and gratitude

Spring Processional: Encounters with a Waking World

Emergence:

Renewal:

Resilience:

Preface

In every wild and open space, the natural world inspires hearts and challenges minds. Secrets wait to be unveiled. Mysteries beg to be solved. Discoveries ignite curiosity. In the pages that follow, I invite you to join me in rambling through forests, fields, and wetlands as they awaken in spring, a season teeming with hope.

Spring begins as a season of awakening. In mid-February, there are subtle clues heralding its imminent arrival. Resident songbirds, including chickadees, titmice, and cardinals, engage in springtime melodies while the woodpeckers tap out a percussive counterpart. By the first week of March, early wildflowers, skunk cabbage and lesser celandine color wetlands and forests. Small depressions fill with water hosting amphibians, aquatic insects, and translucent fairy shrimp. Flocks of blackbirds return to our yards, the males flashing yellow and red epaulets at the muted brown females.

In early April, before the canopy trees get their leaves, the forest floor shimmers with light, quickening the growth of spring ephemerals. Hepatica petals bloom in white, pink, lavender, and purple. Spring beauties dot the ground displaying tiny white petals each with pink stripes. Insect pollinators feast on the nectar of bloodroot, columbine, and Virginia bluebells. Migrating birds fill the forest with song and the flutter of wings in late April and early May. In Pennsylvania alone, twenty-seven species of warblers stop to rest and feed among the trees, each with its own distinctive color pattern and song.

During the final weeks of spring, the forest floor, now shadowed by canopy trees, is home to shade tolerant wildflowers including Canada mayflower, sweet cicely, and dame's rocket. Fields and meadows, hum with the activity of insects visiting wildflowers they pollinate in the bargain. Ponds and wetlands resonate with the calls of frogs. Earlier spring days were filled with the high-pitched trills of American toads. We are now treated to an interspecific amphibian chorus featuring the bullfrog's bagpipe-like drone and the green frog's banjo plucking twang.

The plants and animals in this book can be found throughout the Mid-Atlantic, New England and mid-western states. The exception is the horseshoe crab, found along the Atlantic and Gulf coasts. The timing of events differs from south to north, influenced by a host of variables including elevation, lakeshore effect, proximity to the sea, and climate change. My hope is that these essays encourage you to head out on your own adventure in a park, nature preserve, or even your own backyard. There are always discoveries at hand, wonders to be found.

The First Wildflower

"Whoa—what's this?" Backs bent, boots sinking, my students are mystified by the purple hood with the yellow ball inside. "Spring is on its way," I exclaim. "The skunk cabbage is up!"

It had been a cold winter and we were all eager to get outside and check for any sign that spring was coming. It is usually during the first week of March, that we pull on our boots, layer up with coats, hats and mittens and head out. On our way, we walk past a small swamp at the edge of our hockey field. As we approach, there it is, the first flowering plant of the year breaking through the muddy ground. Though it might be freezing and patches of snow remain on the ground, the skunk cabbage comes up like clockwork. Its tiny shoots make their first appearance in fall. These remain intact during the harshest winter weather, beginning new growth in late February. In these final weeks of winter, skunk cabbage reveals its flower. Imaginations racing, my students examine the unusual floral structure, sharing theories and posing questions.

The skunk cabbage is a member of the Arum family, a group composed largely of tropical plants. We are familiar with some of its houseplant relatives including the philodendrons which decorate many of our homes. A curious flower arrangement, characteristic of these plants, is the lack of petals or sepals. They feature a spike of tiny compact florets, called the spadix, which is surrounded by a shield-like canopy, called

9

the spathe. One member of this family, the krubi of the Sumatran rain forest, bears a spadix eight and a half feet tall, one of the largest floral cluster in the world.

Over time, the skunk cabbage has carried its tropical heritage to our northern latitudes. The one and only species in the northeast can be found from Nova Scotia south to Virginia and westward to Iowa, the total extent of the eastern deciduous forest. Wherever it finds the right conditions, including depressions in floodplains, the bottom of steep ravines, and areas where water lays heavy in the soil, skunk cabbage can take hold. Other representatives of the Arum family found in North America, calla lily, sweet flag, golden club, arrow arum, and Jack-in-the-pulpit, blossom in the spring or early summer. Skunk cabbage, this earliest of bloomers, stands alone. Amazingly, it accomplishes the feat of flowering in February by producing its own heat. In fact, skunk cabbage maintains a near constant flower temperature of seventy-two degrees Fahrenheit regardless of the surrounding temperature of the air and soil. Able to melt their way through snow and ice, these warm islands of skunk cabbage can be fifty degrees warmer than their surroundings.

While all living tissue absorbs oxygen in the process of respiration, generally only warm-blooded animals respire quickly enough to produce appreciable amounts of heat. Yet, skunk cabbage respires at the rate of a small mammal or bird. In the words of botanist, Roger Knutson, "At air temperatures near freezing, a seemingly inactive skunk cabbage is using oxygen and burning fuel at a rate equal to that of a small shrew or hummingbird."

Heating is most pronounced during the early stages of blooming, occurring in conjunction with the development of pollen and egg cells. As the temperature warms up outside, respiration slows down. Like a centrally heated building, skunk cabbage has both a furnace and a thermostat. The spathe surrounding the spadix contains small, isolated air pockets, serving as effective insulation. It also protects the spadix from rain and snow.

Insects and spiders looking for food and warmth find solace in the early-blooming skunk cabbage. The arrangement is reciprocal since bees, flies, and gnats fertilize the flowers, carrying pollen from one plant to the next. The long-jawed spider considers skunk cabbage to be an ideal hideaway for courtship and mating.

A few years ago, I tried to dig up an entire skunk cabbage plant to show to my classes at school. I will never try this again. A good size plant has an underground stem over a foot long and several inches in diameter. The stem grows only a few millimeters a year, but it must grow five to seven years before the plant is large enough to produce its first spathe and spadix. The root does not taper like a carrot, but branches in every direction and buries itself deep in the soil, deeper than I could possibly probe with my shovel. Remarkably, as the roots grow, they simultaneously pull the stem deeper into the mud while stimulating new growth above ground. The intricacies of these plants continue with the connections made by its rhizomes, or underground plant stems. Rhizomes can be described as creeping rootstalks which develop buds and grow horizontally in all directions. It is impossible to know where one plant ends, and another begins.

Skunk cabbage gets its name from the unpleasant skunk-like scent produced when leaves are damaged. The odor is particularly noticeable if you accidentally crush the huge leaves underfoot. Uninjured plants have a mildly sweet smell. The plant is mentioned in several books on wild edibles, and they all recommend several changes of boiling water prior to eating.

The skunk cabbage at the edge of our hockey field may not impress people the same way as the grandeur of the towering hickory and oak do. Still, skunk cabbage, which has been around a lot longer than its hardy neighbors of the woods, inspires us with its resilience and brilliant green foliage. In an article in the "Journal of Heredity," J. Marion Shull put forth the hypothesis that this hardy plant can endure for centuries. "Thus, it happens that the skunk cabbage that is seen today growing in unpretentiousness in any bog may possibly outrival the sturdiest of oaks in point of age, may not improbably have occupied that very spot long before Columbus set foot on our shores, and may continue there a thousand years or more from now if only the fates be kind." Perhaps this is an exaggeration. Still, the skunk cabbage is certainly a force of nature. A plant that can melt its way through snow and ice, maintain a constant, warm flower temperature in the middle of winter, and provide shelter and food for countless species of insects is worth noticing. And it is one my students will never forget.

Drummer in the Woods

In a nearby park, there is a stand of weather-worn trees stripped of their bark and riddled with holes. It has been a long time since these trees sprouted fresh leaves or new growth. Yet, while walking through this desolate landscape, I heard evidence that spring was on its way.

It is hard to believe that spring could return to a forest of bare trees and beckoning shadows. Still, just when it seems that winter will never leave, spring shows up right on cue. On this day, expecting to hear only the clacking of branches in the stiff winter winds, spring announced its presence via a small woodland dweller.  Glancing in the direction of a percussive rapping sound, I found a hairy woodpecker hard at work on an old hollowed out branch.

Woodpeckers demand our attention in much the same way as a visitor knocking on the front door. The sounds they produce turn our heads to search the limbs of tall trees. Once spotted, it's worth taking the time to watch and mentally record their behavior. If a bird seems a bit impatient, hopping from one place to the next, repeating this behavior in a neighboring tree, chances are it is searching for food. When a male woodpecker hammers loudly in one spot, its sound resonating and repetitive, it can indicate that the woodpecker is busy setting up its territory or looking for a mate. Dead trees, with their hollow limbs, are perfect instruments for broadcasting. When the bird shifts its position, the sound changes pitch, giving voice to a variety of notes. Meanwhile, focused hammering in one spot, wood splinters flying, tells us that nest building is underway.

The hairy woodpecker is a common year-round resident of eastern deciduous forests. Dressed in its striking black and white garb, and approximately nine and a half inches tall, it is often confused with the downy woodpecker whose maximum size is six and a half inches. It is helpful to keep in mind that the hairy features a longer, more substantial bill and pure white outer tail feathers. Fortunately, with both species, it is easy to tell the males from the females. Only the male wears a red cap on the back of the head and nape. Both birds are found throughout North America, except in far northern latitudes.

Like most woodpeckers, the hairy spends much of its life on the side of a dead tree. Its strong feet, with two toes in front and two toes in the back, allow it to grasp and hold onto the bark, while the stiff tail provides additional support. Most of its time is spent looking for insects and grubs beneath the bark. Once found, the hairy uses its tongue, covered with barbs and sticky saliva, to harpoon its food. This remarkable tongue features two rear extensions that reach behind the jaw, go up the back of the skull, over the top of the head, and back down into the woodpecker's right nostril. The hyoid bone, a strong and flexible bone covered with muscle, enables a woodpecker to stretch its tongue out of its beak when it feeds. It can thrust its tongue through tiny tree cavities with impressive speed and agility.

It is amazing that a woodpecker can pound its head against a tree day after day and not suffer any brain damage. Adapted to absorb force and prevent injury, woodpeckers have a larger brain case than other birds, offering protection like our cycling helmets. In addition, specialized muscles and bone structures at the base of the skull act like shock absorbers, cushioning each blow and directing most of the energy to the rest of the body. Toes locked into the bark with stiff tail feathers carefully propped in support, the woodpecker has the perfect tools to get the job done.

I stood still and listened to the persistent sound produced by this master of percussion and wished him luck in his upcoming spring endeavors, including finding a mate. Watching and listening to all his activity set me to thinking about warmer spring days ahead that would replace the bleak and windswept landscape before me. I'm up for that. I think the woodpecker and I are both ready for a change.

Night of the Amphibians

They're back! Every year an extraordinary event takes place with few witnesses. Under the cover of darkness, frogs and salamanders emerge from the seemingly lifeless earth and head to temporary woodland pools to join others of their species in a rite of spring. Following in the footsteps of their ancestors, they have made this pilgrimage for thousands of years.

Photo by Craig Newberger

Their destination might be a drainage ditch, a rut along a trail, or perhaps a shallow depression in the forest filled with water. Formed by melting snow and spring rains, these watery places are referred to as vernal pools or temporary wetlands. They are a refuge for frogs and salamanders along with a variety of invertebrate species. These temporary pools dry up soon after the frogs and salamanders move to the land. Fish, turtles, and other predators cannot survive in an area that is wet only a portion of the year.

I'll never forget my first encounter with these extraordinary creatures. One morning during the first week of March, I woke up before dawn to the sound of rain on the rooftop. The temperature was above forty degrees Fahrenheit, seemingly warm enough for frogs and salamanders to appear. While my wife and daughter were still asleep, I quietly crept out of the house and drove to a known trailhead by the local creek.

Walking in the pouring rain, I scanned every water-filled rut and gully for amphibian activity. Unfortunately, there wasn't a frog or salamander in sight.

Later that same day, I returned to resume my search. As it was still raining hard, every wet depression along the trail held promise; however, the temperature was hovering in the low forties which was not quite warm enough. Disappointed for the second time, I headed back home to spend the rest of the day indoors. I involved myself in other projects to help pass the time, and didn't realize that the temperature had risen.

At exactly 8:12 in the evening, I couldn't wait any longer. I grabbed my headlamp, put on my raincoat, slipped into a pair of boots, and headed out the door. When I stepped outside, I noticed the temperature change. All right! For years, I've heard about the "big event." Tonight was the night. I could feel it in my bones.

I headed straight to the vernal pools I had examined earlier in the morning. Once again, they were still. I walked on, shining my headlamp in the water-filled ditch. To the left of the trail, I heard a noise that sounded like the quacking of ducks. Wood Frogs! I could hear them all around me. Hoping to see them, I stepped closer. Silence! Taking their cue, I stood still using my headlamp to search the area. Moments later, there they were! Hundreds of pairs of blue jewels sparkled on the surface of the water. I was spellbound. What an extraordinary sight. Although they had stopped singing, their eyeshine revealed their presence. Remaining still, I waited as the frogs resumed their calls, no longer concerned by my presence.

One of the smallest frogs in this area, the wood frog is generally less than three inches long. Its key field mark is a black mask through the eyes, not seen on any other creature. While other amphibians burrow deep underground to escape winter's cold, the wood frog spends the winter frozen solid in the leaf litter. It manages to resist cell damage and death by keeping ice crystals outside the cell walls. To further its survival, the wood frog has natural antifreeze compounds in its body. Amazingly, they live as far north as Labrador and Alaska. The males, which are smaller and darker than the females, are first to emerge. As soon as they get in the water, they sing non-stop, hoping to wake up the females, who are reddish in color. When the females arrive, there is mass pandemonium in the water. Male wood frogs jump on anything that moves, including other males, salamanders, a floating stick, or if he is lucky, a female. The male clasps the female's waist with his sticky thumb pads, and if the female is ready, she will swim with the male to a sunken branch and release hundreds of tiny black eggs. These are held together in shapeless jelly-like egg masses that often turn green when taking on algae. Typically, you will find several egg masses in one location as they tend to lay their eggs in communal nesting areas. The egg masses in the center are warmed by the surrounding masses and develop quicker than the ones at the edges.

Watching these wood frogs engage in their springtime ritual was all I needed to warm me up on this cold wet evening. Still, there was more. Occasionally, I would glimpse bright yellow polka dots moving through the water. I instantly knew that I was looking at spotted salamanders. One of three species of mole salamanders that live in this area, the spotted salamander is

Photo by Craig Newberger

a remarkable sight. For most of the year, this eight to nine-inch black salamander with large yellow spots lies hidden beneath a rotting log or deep in an underground burrow. As winter fades and spring approaches, rain and melting snow seep through the earth, prompting the spotted salamanders to emerge and return to their birthplace.

Thrilled that I had seen several spotted salamanders in addition to the wood frogs, I headed back to the trailhead feeling lucky. Then, something drew my eye to the right side of the trail. There, in a tiny ditch, were hundreds of spotted salamanders swimming over and around each other, rubbing noses together, and gently stroking each other in what resembled an aquatic ballet. I have since learned that there is a special term for this extraordinary salamander choreography, "Liebesspiel," the German word for lovemaking.

Bending down for a closer look, I noticed there were tiny yellow specks spread like confetti on sticks, leaves, and underwater debris. These were sperm packets, or spermatophores, deposited by the male salamanders. When ready, the female crawls over the spermatophores, picks them up with the lips of her cloaca, and draws them inside her body to fertilize her eggs.

I returned to my house at 2:00 a.m., exhausted with visions of frenzied frogs and dancing salamanders swirling round in my head. Lying in bed, I kept thinking about this truly remarkable natural phenomenon. So many factors had to be in place for these animals to find each other at just the right time: temperature requirements, moisture levels, seasonal processes, temporary pools of water, and acres of naturally forested land. Time sensitive and fragile, these little beings were at risk. I started worrying about all the people that might unwittingly walk and ride that same trail in the morning potentially disturbing the egg masses. A horse or mountain bike could splash through one of their breeding pools crushing some of the animals and sending fertilized eggs flying. Well-meaning maintenance workers might "improve" the trail and fill their habitat with soil and gravel. By the way, was that a 'For Sale' sign I saw on the wooded property adjacent to the trail? Frogs and salamanders winter on this property before they descend to the breeding pools. Would those trees still be there in another year?

A few nights later, I returned to the trail. The temperature had dropped, and the night was surprisingly quiet. I shined my flashlight on the breeding pools and, sure enough, the frogs and salamanders were still out in force. One thing was different though. Everywhere I looked, there were large masses of jelly-like eggs each with a tiny black dot in the middle. When I returned a month later, in April, the ditches along the trail were teaming with tadpoles and salamander larvae. Once again, the frogs and salamanders had successfully completed their annual ritual.

Ever since that first encounter, rainy nights in March make me restless. When the temperature approaches forty-five degrees Fahrenheit, I position my raingear by the door, listen to weather reports and check the batteries in my headlamp. At the first sounds of drenching rain, I head for the trail.

Poetry on Wings

Along with rainbows, butterflies are iconic symbols of beauty and hope. When a colorful butterfly emerges from a dark chrysalis, it reminds us that personal transformation is possible. In the words of Chuang Tzu, "Just when the caterpillar thought that the world was over, it became a butterfly."

Most butterflies are creatures of summer. Every year, the Xerces Society holds its annual count on July Fourth, when the butterfly population is at its peak. However, there are a few species that emerge in the spring, and the mourning cloak butterfly is out and about before the official end of winter.

Some butterflies overwinter as eggs, while others, like the Baltimore checkerspot, survive the winter as caterpillars asleep in the leaf litter. Several species of swallowtail butterflies spend the winter as chrysalises. The mourning cloak is one of a small number of species that spend the winter sheltering as an adult. During unseasonably warm days in March, or even January or February, you can find them flying around. All winter long, they escape the cold by hiding in tiny crevices or underneath bark. With the onset of spring, they flit from tree to tree in search of a good liquid meal. Using their tongues or proboscides, they dine on the risen sap from the stumps of fresh cut trees or sap found on maple twigs gnawed by squirrels.

Like all insects, the mourning cloak has six legs, but the first pair is underdeveloped, placing it in the family of "four-footed" butterflies. Its three-inch wings are notably notched, which explains its membership in the "anglewing" tribe. Seen from above, the purplish black wings are dotted with blue spots and lined with a rim of yellow. Seen from below, the wings are dull brown with tiny threads of black. When folded

19

above the back, the mourning cloak looks more like a fragment of dead wood than a living insect. The butterfly's ability to camouflage itself is heightened when it remains motionless. Most predators are only motivated by moving prey.

Few insects are as entertaining to watch, especially during moments of courtship. The male and female engage in a series of short chases, sometimes taking the form of spiral flights. The two butterflies spiral to a height of twenty or thirty feet, when suddenly one butterfly plummets headfirst to the ground.

It is believed that a butterfly cannot recognize another member of its species until they are about a foot away. Driven by the urge to mate, the male mourning cloak will chase anything small that flies. It is not unusual to find one in pursuit of the wrong species. When he realizes his mistake, he will quickly back off and fly elsewhere.

The female lays tiny clusters of eggs around the twigs of elm, willow, and poplar. The eggs hatch in ten to twelve days and immediately the tiny black caterpillars crawl to the nearest leaf to eat. Like other caterpillars, they feast on the surface of green leaves, leaving the fine network of veins undisturbed.

Those that survive the appetite of predators eventually hang from a twig and enclose themselves in hardened tan chrysalises lined with a double row of spikes. In June and July, the newly hatched Mourning Cloaks emerge. In southern states, there are often three broods a year, but in New England and the Mid-Atlantic states, there are usually two. The final brood will achieve adulthood in October or November and overwinter in this stage.

Along with returning birds and emerging wildflowers, the mourning cloaks are a welcome sign of spring. When most of the natural world is still fast asleep, they fly and court and sun themselves with open wings. They herald the beginning of the butterfly season and the promise of warmer days ahead.

Drama in the Field

"Nature within her inmost self divides
To trouble men with having to take sides."
–Robert Frost

Courtships are the spice of spring. In woods, fields, ponds and marshes, animal activity is on the rise as the task of finding a mate takes center stage. On occasion, I have had the good fortune to watch animals engaged in elaborate courtship rituals. Keeping a discrete distance and all movements in check, I have been able to view fascinating interactions and behaviors.

Unfortunately, I am not always the sole observer of these rituals. Many animals rely on sound traveling significant distances to attract potential mates. They might perform aerial flights, complex dances, or other types of auditory and/or visual displays. In doing so, their typical vigilant surveillance can fall short, making them easy targets for predators. I am reminded of a late afternoon in March when a friend and I hiked out to a field of tall grasses. We had planned our arrival to coincide with the setting of the sun and pending twilight. Perfect timing to watch for male woodcocks engaging in courtship display.

Woodcocks are a rare sight for us. During most of the year, this stout, well-camouflaged bird with an extremely long bill eludes us. Much of the woodcock's life is spent with its outsized beak to the ground, searching for worms and other invertebrates. It blends in flawlessly with the fallen leaves and shadows of the forest floor. Come spring, our opportunities to see them increase significantly. Male woodcocks take to the sky, performing one of the most spectacular rituals I've seen in the natural world.

These rituals or courtship displays begin shortly after sunset, a time when the world quiets and the vibrant colors of day take on subtle gray tones. The male woodcock, seeking to attract a potential mate, receives an element of protection in these low light conditions. Leaving the adjacent woods, he lands in an abandoned field or thicket of grasses.

Bobbing his head, he emits a strident buzzing call known as a "peent." Making a quarter turn, he looks into the distance and again bobs his head and issues a loud peent. Pause. Making the next quarter turn, he issues another peent and so it goes, a series of quarter turns, facing out into the night, each followed by a peent. At a moment of the male's choosing, he takes to the sky.

He may fly as high as three hundred feet in the air, making a series of large sweeping circles encompassing an area several acres wide. Upon descent, his spiraling acrobatic display is further enhanced by a whistling sound. It took years for the scientific community to determine the source of this sound to be the feathers and not the vocal cords. Slow motion photography has captured both visual and auditory recordings of the outer feathers at each wingtip. Air moving through these feathers produces a whistling sound as the woodcock spirals to ground. Shortly before landing, the woodcock emits a soft warbling cry from his throat, sometimes referred to as the "kissing song." Once back in the field, the woodcock repeats his display, complete with the now familiar "peent" throughout the twilight hours.

My friend and I walked through the field until we settled down in a high spot where the dry grasses offered us a good view of the sunset on the horizon. It didn't take long to be rewarded with the familiar peent sound which seemed to be coming from several directions at once. There was more than one woodcock in these fields. This was going to be a great night!

At one point, a bird landed less than fifty feet from us. Through binoculars, we observed the woodcock nodding its head, peenting, and strutting in various directions. After repeating this behavior twice, the bird flew up into the sky, returning in a series of spirals to the same spot in the field. We had not expected to see what happened next.

Within seconds of the woodcock's return, a great-horned owl swooped down on the unwary bird. We felt like we were watching one of those nature documentaries on television. Awestruck, we remained motionless, watching the drama unfold. I was overwhelmed by conflicting emotions. I feared for the woodcock yet marveled at the hunting techniques of the owl. Miraculously the woodcock escaped. It flew a considerable distance away and resumed its courtship ritual as if nothing had happened. When we returned the following night, there was a male woodcock in this same location, carrying out its display undeterred.

I fully understand that the owl and the woodcock are both part of the balance of nature. Yet, truthfully, I was rooting for the woodcock. March evenings would not be the same without the traditional witnessing of the "sky dance." My friend, who had a special interest in birds of prey, was rooting for the owl. Of course, our preferences were not important. Everyone must eat.

An Offensive Defense

On dark nights, when the weather is crisp and clear, I frequently step outside to look at the night sky. During the winter months, there are few distractions, save for the possible hoot of an owl or cry of a fox. Come spring, there are other surprises. On one occasion, my star gazing was interrupted by an unexpected visitor. Standing under the quarter moon, breathing in the scent of thawing soil, I detected another aroma which led me to abandon my nighttime foray.

During most of the year, the striped skunk is seldom seen, heard, or smelled. It rarely travels more than a quarter mile from its burrow. The hot and humid days of summer send the skunk underground, seeking refuge from oppressive temperatures. Likewise, it spends most of the winter months in an underground burrow, emerging on warmer days to search for food. As spring approaches, the skunk travels across woods, fields, lawns, and roadways to find a mate. It is not unusual for a male skunk to travel five miles in search of a partner. The last thing I wanted to do was to interrupt a skunk on its quest.

The skunk, well-endowed with sharp claws and powerful canine teeth, employs strategies unlike other animals. It has found a way of defending itself without ever engaging in battle. Well adapted to survive amongst larger and more vicious creatures in woodland and field, skunks have earned their place in a challenging world.

Long before it was adopted by the military, the skunk developed a system of chemical warfare which is virtually foolproof. Hidden beneath its tail are two large glands containing a powerful liquid musk. By contracting its hip muscles, the musk can be fired at will. Clear and golden-yellow in color, it appears faintly phosphorescent at dusk and creates a deep yellow stain on a small white dog. The active ingredient is thiol, an organic compound containing sulfur. It may cause temporary blindness, coughing, choking, and fainting. While these symptoms may disappear after a short period of time, the smell persists. Weasels and their relatives also possess potent musk glands. However, the skunk's ability to maneuver its glands for self-defense exceeds them all.

The little sharpshooter can fire its musk in any direction simply by twisting its rump towards the target. Contrary to popular belief, it can even shoot its artillery when hoisted by the tail. On a typical day, the spray will travel between ten and twelve feet. Prevailing winds sometimes carry it a lot farther. The skunk is capable of firing five or six rounds before running out of ammunition. Of course, it does everything possible to avoid getting to this point. It takes about a week for a refill, leaving the skunk virtually defenseless in the meantime.

Whenever possible, the skunk will give fair warning. When confronted, a skunk will stamp its forefeet on the ground and emit a series of shrill-sounding hisses. If this warning fails to frighten the predator away, it will arch its back and raise its tail. Young and inexperienced predators who goad a skunk suffer distressing consequences long after. Most adult animals will quickly retreat to avoid being sprayed.

Lacking a sense of smell, great horned owls are not deterred by the ultimate defense of the skunk. Additionally, the owl's eyes are protected by a nictitating membrane. This membrane covers the eye, acting as a shield, rendering any liquid which reaches its eyes harmless. It is the only known animal that will eat a live skunk.

There is one other swift-moving predator accountable for the demise of many a wandering skunk. Every year, especially in early spring, millions of skunks are killed by the deadliest of all predators, *Automobilis fatalis*. The skunk has not evolved to make distinctions between a cornfield and a highway. Instead, it carries out its daily tasks with the same intent in either place.

As I reached the door of my house, I felt a sense of relief that I had not encountered what I had smelled. I paused to consider how many new and emerging creatures would soon show up in my yard. I would try again another night to view the twinkling stars and glowing planets in the night sky. It was time to give this night back to the skunk whose perfume lingered in the air.

Evening Symphony

Listen. You can hear the music a mile away cutting through the silent night, high notes soaring. A symphony of sound emanates from wetlands where winter temperatures once quieted the landscape. Pulsating in pitch and rhythm, the dynamics shift from pianissimo to forte and back again. It starts with the singing of one tiny frog, not much larger than your thumbnail. Joined by countless others, their choral resonance soon dominates the landscape. This is what I have been waiting for. This is the voice of spring.

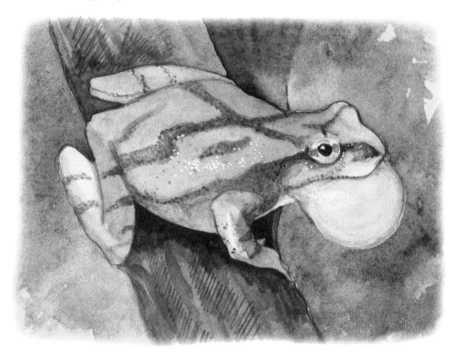

Seasonal sounds often serve as background music during walks in the park, at the beach or on a bike path. Birds chirping and insects buzzing become commonplace as our attention focuses on the visual world. Yet these minute singers, spring peepers, issue a call that demands to be heard both in its intensity and uniqueness.

For many years I listened to these mysterious vocalists. On those occasions, it never occurred to me that tiny singing frogs could make that much sound. You might think that it would be easy to locate them once heard. It is not. It takes patience and discipline to find them among the reeds, grasses, and remnants of the past winter thaw.

I spent many years looking for spring peepers before I saw one. Whenever I walked up to a pond filled with singing peepers, they instantly quieted, making it impossible to know where to look. The trick, I found, was to stay perfectly still in one spot. Breathe and listen. One lone peeper begins to sing. Tentatively a few more join until their sound reaches a resounding crescendo.

Resuming my search to see a peeper in action, I shine my flashlight around the water's edge. I begin moving ever so slowly and carefully in the direction of the loudest calls. I do my best to cause minimal disturbance and avoid the possibility of footfalls injuring any choral members. I can usually track down a few singing peepers if I employ patience as my guide. On a good night, I may see five or six singing peepers, although I know there are many more surrounding me. One scientist estimates there could be 1500 peepers concentrated in a single acre of breeding marsh.

Spring peepers can be heard all day long, though they are considerably louder after sundown. In late March or early April, they emerge from beneath the leaf litter and head to the temporary pools and marshes where they were born. Like wood frogs and spotted salamanders, spring peepers depend on these temporary depressions or vernal pools, which collect and hold water during spring only to dry up by mid-summer. Vernal pools are the perfect arrangement for animals like spring peepers that begin their lives in the water, moving to dry land as adults. Here they are free to go about their courtship without fear of being eaten by hungry predators found in deeper waters including fish, turtles, and some aquatic mammals.

Equipped with sticky discs on their toes, spring peepers are well-adapted for climbing trees and shrubs. Most of the year, they are almost impossible to find. They are hidden in the leaf litter or up in the trees as silent sentinels. It is the coming of spring that moves them to disclose their presence as they return to the water to perpetuate their species.

When the male frog sings, he takes air into his vocal sac, which swells, resembling a giant bubble or balloon. At its fullest, this vocal sac seems larger than the entire body of the frog. This may sound overstated, however a peeper is seldom more than three-quarters of an inch long. Females are slightly larger than males, though never more than an inch and a half long. The male then performs a rapid succession of high bell-like calls, announcing his presence to the females, inviting them to visit his square-foot territory so that he can fertilize their eggs.

Every March, there are wildflowers that bloom before the last snowstorm and birds that come back early to find the ground still frozen. In similar fashion, spring peepers emerge on sporadic warm, wet days only to experience the return of colder temperatures. Like the wildflowers and the birds, spring peepers must adapt to daily changes occurring on the cusp of spring.

In the words of John Burroughs, "The most precious things in life are near at hand, without money and without price." This is how I feel every time I hear the high-pitched calls of spring peepers. Listen.

Ephemerals of Mud Time

"Where flowers bloom, so does hope."
–Ladybird Johnson

Beginning in April, harbingers of spring can be found on every hill and dale. Poet Robert Frost referred to this time of year as "mud time," the time between the swelling of tree buds and the unraveling of blooms and leaves. It is a time of year characterized by dampness in the air, mist rising from the marshes, and the sometimes sweet, sometimes rank smell of fresh moist earth. Late spring overwhelms the senses with the fragrances of lilacs and roses, the music of songbirds, and the prominence of sun. The essence of mud time lays in its promise.

Every year, I look forward to the spring ephemerals. Before the unfurling of leaves on canopy trees and understory shrubs, sunlight penetrates the forest floor, creating the perfect environment for early wildflowers. The flowers of spring ephemerals wither by early May, leaving what is left of their life in underground structures. While true bulbs are found on daffodils, tulips and hyacinths, the spring ephemerals subsist on modified structures for storing energy. Corms are tiny and round or oval in shape. Tubers are thickened and enlarged. In both cases, these serve as primary storage units, providing nutrition for the plant. Rhizomes are swollen stems that grow horizontally under the soil, spreading in all directions.

By the end of March, the forest is awash with spring beauties. When fully open, the flowers consist of five pink and white petals and two sepals. The flowers open on sunny days and close when it is cloudy or dark. They attract a wide variety of bees and other insects. Each fertile flower produces a tiny capsule containing many seeds. The underground tubers of spring beauties are known as wild edibles to many. They taste like potatoes and are known by many local names including fairy potato and mountain potato.

Hepatica, or liver leaf, has five to twelve colorful sepals, which most people assume are petals. The sepals surround tiny green bisexual flowers in the center of the plant. Hepatica flowers can be pink, purple, blue or white. For centuries, many believed, according to the Doctrine of the Signatures, that the shapes of the leaves described the medicinal qualities of plants. Hepatica was thought to be good for the liver due to the three liver-like lobes on the basal leaves.

Bloodroot has one large basal leaf with five to seven lobes. The flower rises from the center of a single curled leaf, opening when lit by the sun and closing in the dark. The leaves and flowers spread from an orange or reddish rhizome, which grows at or slightly below the surface. When the stem is broken, it exudes a red colored liquid from whence the plant gets its common name. In addition to reproduction through rhizomes, bloodroot seeds are collected and spread by ants creeping along the ground.

Bloodroot Photo by Craig Newberger

The trout lily, also known as adder's tongue, grows in large colonies, usually on a sunlit hillside. Most of the plants have one long slender leaf mottled like the scales of a trout. A small number of plants among the masses will have two leaves. Upon close examination you will find that these are the only ones producing the tiny yellow flowers. It takes

31

seven or eight years for the corm to mature and grow deep enough underground for the plant to flower. Therefore, a trout lily in flower is at least seven years old. They can easily live to the ripe old age of twenty.

Common in deciduous forests throughout the northeast, the flowers of wild ginger are one of nature's best kept secrets. Hidden beneath a canopy of heart-shaped leaves, the bell-like purple flowers rest along the ground. While most flowers advertise their presence to pollinating insects, like bees and butterflies, wild ginger is pollinated by flies that emerge from the ground in early spring. When the seeds of wild ginger mature, they are collected by ants who carry them to their underground nests.

Common names like shooting stars, bleeding hearts, and squirrel corn suggest a Lilliputian's Garden of delight. I am reminded repeatedly of an old German folktale in which the young hero traveled everywhere in search of a flower that he had seen in his dreams. When he returned after a long and fruitless quest, he found the object of his dreams growing right at his doorstep. You don't have to travel far to find the simple joys of mud time. A treasure chest of riches lies within close reach, just waiting to be discovered.

Jack and Jill in the Pulpit

My favorite spring ephemeral is the Jack-in-the-pulpit. When I take students for nature walks, my secret agenda is that they discover this plant in full bloom. I look forward to the moment when someone spies the little "person" hiding inside the flower. Everyone stops, squats and jostles to get a closer look. Immediately the questions fly as we engage in a wide-ranging conversation about one of the most captivating wildflowers of spring.

Jack-in-the-pulpit can be found in deciduous forests from southern Canada to the Gulf of Mexico. It is a member of the Arum family, with 114 genera and 3,750 known species. Although most diverse in the tropics and the Mediterranean region, there are several species of Arum in the United States, including the prolific skunk cabbage.

These visually unique plants capture our imaginations with their unusual flowers. The singular bloom on its own stalk resembles the shape of a pulpit in a church. A shield-shaped green and maroon striped spathe covers the pulpit and serves as an umbrella preventing water from filling the flower.

It is what lies beneath the spathe that my young students and I find irresistible. Gently lifting the spathe, heads bump together as everyone wants to get a good look at Jack … or Jill. This columnar structure inside the pulpit, I tell them, is called the spadix.

Jack-in-the-pulpit first flowers as a male, transitioning from male to female or female to male, throughout its lifespan of twenty-five years or more. This is not a change left to chance, rather it is a survival strategy employed by the plant. A Jack-in-the-pulpit develops into a female when the corm, or root-storage structure, can provide the necessary stored resources to support flower and fruit production. When stored resources become depleted, the plant will revert to being male or a non-flowering plant. During months of optimal growth conditions, more females prevail. The reverse is also true. When conditions are lacking, male plants dominate. Factors contributing to changes in a female's corm size include soil moisture and nutrients, weather, and a variety of invertebrates who may feast on the leaves.

There are several features to consider when determining if a plant is male or female. Males appear to have three leaves, resembling poison ivy to the casual observer. Jack-in-the-Pulpit's single compound leaf rises from the soil as a stalk ending with three leaflets, while poison ivy has three separate leaves on a stem which is attached to a woody vine. The female plant, our Jill-in-the-pulpit, grows larger and has two stalked leaves each with three leaflets. At the base of the female spadix are tiny green flowers with white centers. In the summer when these mature, they will form fleshy green berries that will turn bright red in fall. The flowers at the base of the male spadix are small, pale pollen-laden flowers.

Jack-in-the-pulpit requires its pollinators to carry pollen from male to female plants. Unlike showy flower blossoms which bees and butterflies prefer, the flowers of Jack-in-the-pulpit are difficult to access. To solicit pollinators, the spadix emits a fungus-like odor which attracts fungus gnats. If the tiny gnats visit a male plant, they can easily find their way inside the bloom. Finding their way out requires greater effort. The slippery sides of the spathe make it almost impossible for gnats to crawl upward, sending the gnats tumbling down to the bottom. If they are lucky, they will find a tiny opening or "escape hatch" at the base of the spathe. Having repeatedly brushed against pollen heavy flowers in their quest to depart, the fungus gnats become loaded with pollen. Some of the same gnats land on female plants, where the pollen grains drop onto the female flowers found at the base of the spadix.

Unfortunately, once a fungus gnat enters the spathe of a female there is no way out. They remain trapped and die. For years, Jack-in-the-pulpit was considered a carnivorous plant; however, it does not consume the gnats like a pitcher plant. If the pollen is successfully transferred, at significant cost to the gnats, the female flowers will be fertilized, producing a cluster of berries.

In the temporal world of spring ephemerals, flowers appear briefly in April and are gone by May. The leaves remain a short time longer capturing energy from the sun to store in their corms for next year. Lacking in color and fragrance, Jack-in-the-pulpit stands out for its floral structure and its unique and effective method to ensure its propagation for future generations.

My students and I have had a successful walk. Among the rewards of an afternoon on the trail, they have discovered a world of relationships and possibilities. I, on the other hand, have both achieved my agenda and witnessed priceless moments of awareness and connection.

Hope Within Reach

"Hope is the thing with feathers."
–Emily Dickinson

Soaring to 150 feet, circling high in the sky, or plunging into water for a fish, osprey are impressive birds to behold. Whenever I see or hear an osprey, I have to stop and watch. Sometimes referred to as fish hawks and often confused with eagles, osprey have distinctive field marks. The white underside and conspicuous crook in their wings set them apart from eagles. A black eye stripe, absent in eagles, runs from the beak to the back of the head. Formidable raptors, their wingspan of four to six feet allows them to cover a wide area and descend at considerable speed.

For years, I've been fascinated by the osprey's superb hunting technique. Target in sight, the osprey hovers and prepares to strike. Drawing its wings back, the osprey takes on the aerodynamic shape of a javelin. Plunging toward its prey, talons thrust forward, the osprey hits the water, sinks, and rises with a fish. An osprey's four talons are arranged three in the front and one in the back. The bottoms of the toes are covered with needle-sharp spines. Its unique ability to rotate its outer talon backwards, placing two toes in front and two toes in the rear, ensures a secure grip on slippery prey. Lifting off from the water, the osprey locks the fish in a streamlined headfirst position, reducing wind resistance.

In the late 1970s, I lived in a house overlooking the Westport River, not far from the Adamsville, Rhode Island town center. Along the two branches of the river, osprey were a common sight, and their numbers were increasing. It wasn't always this way. I had the good fortune to meet and volunteer with Gil and Jo Fernandez who spent years banding birds and keeping census and behavioral records. They built tall nesting platforms and set them up along the string of small islands that dot the river. These platforms were adopted by mated pairs who built nests and raised young. The efforts of Gil, Jo and the volunteers demonstrate the importance of individual actions.

Every morning in mid-March, I would walk along the West Branch, keeping an eye out for the first returning osprey. Invariably, a bird could be seen by the first or second day of spring. First to arrive were the males, preceding the females by several days. Their return seemed to coincide with that of the alewives who were returning from the sea to the rivers. Flying from Central and South America, the osprey returned year after year to the same nest, which they continued to enlarge and repair.

One year, in late March, I noticed several nesting platforms out in the river had fallen during our winter storms. I called Gil Fernandez and together we repaired the platforms and set them back up. As we rowed back to shore in our boat, we were rewarded by the sighting of an osprey landing on one of the platforms.

Many birds of prey, including the osprey, suffered severely from the use of DDT, a synthetic insecticide developed in the 1940s. It was used to combat insect borne diseases such as malaria. After WWII, this "miracle pesticide" was heavily used by farmers to prevent insect damage to crops. With a half-life of fifteen years, DDT concentrates in the fatty tissue of animals. As it travels up the food chain, the accumulation of the chemical increases, posing serious health consequences to the animals that ingest it. It becomes most dangerous to the health of predatory animals at the top of the food chain. In adult female birds, DDT inhibits the amount of calcium available for proper shell development. As a result, osprey were laying tissue-thin eggs, which would crack when the parents sat on them, thus producing few to any offspring during a nesting season. In 1972, DDT was banned in the United States. Since that time, the osprey population has increased dramatically.

In 1973, when the United States congress passed the Endangered Species Act, the osprey was placed on the list of federally protected wildlife. Although today they are still listed as imperiled or threatened in some states, they have made a significant comeback. In fact, I frequently see osprey flying over our school campus in southeastern Pennsylvania.

All animals have habitat requirements and osprey require a large body of water with tall trees adjacent. Serving as hunting perches, the branches of dead or live trees are also used for nesting. Their nests are clumsy looking structures, made of long sticks, often driftwood, mixed with anything at hand, including bones, cloth, old shoes, and other pieces of clothing. The nest is lined with softer materials, such as seaweed or moss.

Osprey mate for life, with courtship occurring every spring. Flying excitedly overhead and making lots of noise, both sexes chase each other, soaring, whirling, and engaging in a variety of acrobatics. Before mating takes place, the male calls to the female. When she responds, he brings her an offering of food, fluffs out his feathers, and performs a variety of displays and postures. This behavior attracts her attention and prepares her to mate.

The female sits on her creamy white eggs with brown spots for twenty-five to thirty days, while the male catches fish. He occasionally relieves her on the nest or stands guard nearby, watching for predators. Their eggs hatch in early June and the young remain in the nest for up to two months. When they are seven weeks old, they begin their first test flights, and at the ripe old age of eight or nine weeks, they are ready to leave the nest. The parents head south a month before their children, giving the young time to practice flying before their long journey. Birds banded in the northeastern United States have been recovered as far away as Venezuela. The young stay down south for three or four years, and each spring thereafter return north to breed.

Several summers ago, as an instructor at the National Audubon Society's educator's camp on Hog Island in Maine, I arrived to find that an osprey pair had set up a nest on the camp's peninsula. There had been a growing number of osprey nesting on the adjacent islands, including the more remote parts of Hog Island for many years. This year, the birds had constructed a large nest right behind the camp workshop between one of the cabins and the dining hall. The surprising location of this nest made birding enthusiasts dreams come true. The osprey had a perfect view of Muscongus Bay and we had stellar views of them. Both the male and the female made frequent flights out into the bay to fill the hungry bellies of the three young in the nest. Every morning before breakfast, spotting scopes and binoculars were locked in position. SLR camera motors hummed while iPhones and Androids clicked. Every day was a good day to observe this pair and their young. The following year, it got even better.

By the time I arrived, Explore.org had combined its technology with the Audubon Camp staff and volunteers to livestream the activity in the nest. This made it possible for campers to have breakfast with the birds every morning. In between bites of blueberry pancakes and sips of coffee, educators would keep their eyes trained on the large screen TV in the dining hall. Cheers of support or groans of dismay would fill the room when chicks would grab their pieces of fish or be tackled by a hungry sibling. Throughout the day, campers would check between classes to see what might be going on in the nest. What an opportunity! Through this new online lens and the Hog Island social media pages, campers and the public alike were able to follow the daily events of this mated pair from nesting to fledging. The use of this type of media to assist us in creating awareness and gathering information is invaluable to supporting the needs of these birds.

Nesting platforms, the banning of DDT, education, and laws to preserve wetland areas have made a big difference. Since the late 1970s, the osprey population has been on the rise. They are one of many conservation success stories. It is possible to craft policies and practices that support species in danger. I have seen it happen.

Living a Double Life

Hidden from public view, most salamanders spend their lives concealed in leaf litter, beneath rocks or fallen limbs, or underwater in ponds, lakes, vernal pools, and streams. Many species are rare or uncommon. Others are surprisingly plentiful, like the red-backed salamander, the most common vertebrate in the world. Scientists estimate there can be several thousand in one acre of mature deciduous forest, but you will not see one unless you turn over rocks and logs.

The red eft is the notable exception to this rule. Colored Halloween orange, this is an animal that advertises its presence. To add to its allure, its back is peppered with tiny black flecks and larger crimson spots with black borders. The eyes are particularly striking with an elongated black band across a golden background. On rainy or foggy days, the eft emerges from its hiding place to forage for insects, worms, and other  small critters. On one occasion, following a significant downpour, my students counted over three hundred efts in a half hour period. This was an exciting task made all the easier as the efts wandered the forest floor in plain sight. Seemingly fearless, red efts possess a defense strategy similar to monarch butterflies and poison dart frogs. Their bright orange coloration warns potential predators to stay away or suffer the consequences of contacting the poisonous toxin they secrete through their skin.

A small animal, the red eft is seldom more than two inches from head to flattened tail, which it uses to turn itself over if it ends up on its back.

The legs and feet are short and far apart, but the eft can move swiftly when the ground is wet. For years, I found them in the forest without knowing their backstory. The red eft is the juvenile and terrestrial stage in the life cycle of a red-spotted newt. Living life in distinct stages, the newt begins its existence in a pond or stream, spends its juvenile years as a red eft on land, and returns to the water as an adult.

I have often been asked to explain the difference between a salamander and a newt. One is a subset of the other. All newts are salamanders, but not all salamanders are newts. Over the course of their lives, newts divide their time between aquatic and terrestrial habitats. There are several species of newts in the Gulf region and the Pacific Northwest, but the red-spotted newt is the only one in the northeast. It is possible to view this remarkable creature during every one of the four seasons. I'll never forget watching these unusual amphibians swimming and foraging in a beaver pond during an early thaw. At that time of year, the cold water is highly oxygenated, and the newts take in oxygen through their skins. I even observed them swimming underneath the ice. Colored green above and yellow below, they look nothing like the terrestrial efts. The only thing they have in common are the tiny black dots and the larger red ones, still bordered with black. Streamlined for swimming, they range in size from two to four inches across from head to tail. The long tail serves as both a propeller and a rudder to steer it through the water.

Breeding begins in late winter or early spring. The male, distinguished by his keeled tail and swollen feet and hind legs, waves his tail and wiggles, emitting pheromones, a special perfume to attract females. Attracted by his movement and fragrant aroma, the female allows the male to hold onto her using his hind legs as they thrash around in the water in a courtship embrace. Upon release, the male swims ahead of the female and deposits his spermatophores, which are picked up by the female.

While most amphibians lay their eggs in jelly-like masses, female newts lay single eggs coated with jelly. In a week, she will attach three or four hundred eggs to the aquatic vegetation, though only a small number survive predators and other environmental factors. Depending on water temperature, the eggs hatch in three to five weeks, becoming tiny larva less than a half inch long. Perfectly adapted for life in the water, the larvae breathe with feathery gills.

Metamorphosis takes place in mid to late summer, after three or four months as aquatic larvae. The juvenile newts, now called red efts, move out of the water to dry land, replete with lungs, legs, eyelids, and bright orange or red coloration. They may travel vast distances to find a place to call home. After sleeping through the winter beneath rocks, decaying logs, or leaf litter, they can be seen out and about in spring, summer, and fall. Recent studies indicate that the red eft stage might last twelve to fifteen years. As they mature, they undergo another transformation, changing shape and color, yet retaining their lungs. Preparations completed, they return to the water body of their birth as aquatic adults. Their ability to begin life in the water, physically adapt to live on land for years, and then return to the water is extraordinary.

Kneeling on the forest floor, watching the red-efts crawl to unknown destinations, we become a captive audience. One of my students leans forward, gently picking up an eft in her moist and soiled hand. Bringing the eft to eye level, her eyes widen as her smile broadens. She has connected. I am delighted.

Sparks in the Forest

Waves of tiny brightly colored songbirds fly overhead. Multi-colored lights flash by as they dart back and forth at record-breaking speeds. The warblers are back! In woods and fields pausing for mere moments, they lift off in a feathered frenzy, seizing our attention with their jewel-tone colors. Flashing yellow rumps, blue backs, orange wing patches, black hoods, and chestnut sides, they are about the serious business of building up their energy stores. While small flocks of warblers return north beginning in April, most of them arrive in early May. Travelers by night, they spend their days catching insects and readying for important reproduction tasks soon to follow.

When I share a sighting with someone, they often express delight followed closely by surprise. "Does this happen every year?" Watching the quick movements of the warblers, we make observations and talk about where they might have been all winter, what they are searching for and where they might be headed next. Once seen, it is hard to forget their inexhaustible energy and their flashes of color.

I first became attuned to warblers when I was camping in southern New Hampshire. Sleeping under the stars, I awoke around 5:00 a.m. on a May morning to the greatest profusion of bird song I had ever heard in my life. I jumped out of my sleeping bag and raced to the car to grab my binoculars. Warblers seemed to be everywhere at once. Small slender-billed birds flitted from branch to branch. Sunrise intensified the tiny patches of color on their bodies. I couldn't stop looking. I was hooked.

There are over fifty species of warblers in North America and more than half of them can be seen passing through the northeast. We have given them common names that describe their field marks including chestnut-sided warbler, black-throated blue warbler, black-throated green warbler, black and white warbler, yellow warbler, yellow-rumped warbler, hooded warbler, American redstart, cerulean warbler and so on. Interestingly, the prothonotary warbler, with its yellow head and breast was named after the yellow papal robes of Catholic clerks.

Warbler identification takes time and patience. Birds moving swiftly between one tree and the next are difficult to find using your eyes alone. I have found that if you stay in one spot and listen for their sounds, you can more easily zero in on their location. Combining visual and auditory tools provides a better chance for identification. Learning birdsong using recordings available on websites or apps is very useful when looking for and identifying warblers. When I first hear the warblers each year, I feel like old friends have come to visit. Some warbler sounds I easily recognize: the chestnut-sided warbler's "Please please, pleased to meet cha"; the common yellowthroat's "Wichity Wichity Wichity"; and the yellow warbler's "Sweet sweet sweet I'm so sweet." One of my favorites, the prairie warbler, sings "Zee Zee Zee Zee Zee" up the chromatic scale.

It is also helpful to recognize behavioral characteristics associated with certain warblers. The black and white warbler hangs upside down like a nuthatch, incessantly circling the trunks of trees in search of insects in the crevices of the bark. The ovenbird and the northern waterthrush are usually found low to the ground, searching for insects beneath the leaf litter. Others fly at tremendous speeds, catching insects on the wing.

There are many outstanding places to experience warbler migration, including Magee Marsh Wildlife Area in Ohio, Central Park in New York City, the Mount Auburn Cemetery in Cambridge, Massachusetts, Carpenter's Woods in Philadelphia, and the Beech Forest on Cape Cod. The geographic location of Magee Marsh Wildlife Area makes it a perfect staging area or migration trap. Sitting right up against the south side of Lake Erie, it serves the many requirements of a traveling bird. Central Park and Mount Auburn Cemetery share common features which attract huge flocks of warblers. These sizable green spaces within cities are also along established flyways the birds use to migrate.

On Cape Cod, the Beech Forest in the Provincelands is a great place for viewing warblers. Before taking the big step and flying out over Cape Cod Bay or the mighty Atlantic Ocean, large concentrations of warblers stop and feed along the margins of this forest of beech and oak. I have spent many spring mornings walking the sandy pathways to see how many species had gathered. On one occasion, when I pulled up to the parking lot, it was filled with cars jammed tightly together. Oddly, I didn't see a single person and I couldn't find any warblers. Eventually, I ran into a couple who told me that everything was happening at the steps by the edge of the pond. Sure enough, when I arrived at the pond, there were warblers galore. I counted ten different species. A woman, who stood there for three hours, told me she had counted twenty-two species.

In Philadelphia, the Wissahickon Gorge is an exceptional place to find warblers. It is one of the largest natural areas located in a city. Surrounded by urban development, the warblers are concentrated into this natural oasis of forest, stream, and wetlands. On one occasion when I joined the Wyncote Audubon Society for a walk in the Carpenter's Woods section, we saw seventeen species of warblers.

The length of migration varies with the species. The pine warbler travels a comparatively short distance, from the southern United States to New England. The blackpoll warbler migrates from the tropics of South America to Canada. During spring migration, the males arrive brightly colored and easy to identify. Over the summer their plumage dulls and becomes less distinct which makes identification more difficult in fall.

At night, they travel in mixed flocks with numbers that baffle the imagination, guided by the light of the moon and stars and their personal GPS systems. When conditions are just right, it is possible to witness migration against the silhouette of a full moon.

The short-lived days of peak migration wane as the first official day of summer nears. Leaves, hidden in buds during the winter, burst hard shell coverings to shadow the forest floor. Where sunlight once flooded the tender spring ephemerals of March, April and early May, dried stalks and seedpods are all that remain. Many of the warblers continue their journey northward in concert with the seasonal changes. Some stay to nest and raise their young. We are thankful that our garden flowers have begun to bloom and anticipate the fruits that summer will yield. And we will need to wait another year for the next spectacle of sparks in the forest.

Playing Possum

Many years ago, when I worked at the Cape Cod Museum of Natural History, a woman arrived with a box of helpless baby opossums. The mother had been hit by a car and killed, leaving behind four young survivors inside her pouch. When we looked inside the box, we saw that the babies were covered with fur and their eyes were open. Young at this stage of development are at least two months old, almost ready to leave the pouch. We nurtured and fed them, first baby formula in an eye dropper and later cat food and leftover produce. When they no longer needed our care, we released them on the grounds of the museum. Our time spent interacting with the young opossums allowed us the opportunity to observe these rarely seen nocturnal mammals.

Opossums are the only marsupial, or pouch-bearing mammal, found in North America. There are no marsupials native to Europe, Asia, or Africa though close to seventy percent of the mammals on the Australian continent are pouch-bearers. In this remote corner of the world, a host of relatives of the opossum thrive, including kangaroos, wallabies, bandicoots, Tasmanian devils, and koalas. Marsupials lie midway in evolution between the primitive egg-laying monotremes, such as the duck-billed platypus and the spiny anteater, and the higher placental mammals. They give birth to live young who continue their development in a specially equipped pouch. Millions of years ago, when the positioning of the continents differed from their current location,

marsupials roamed over all the land masses. In 1820, Georges Cuvier, a French naturalist and biologist, discovered marsupial fossils in the gypsum of the streets of Paris.

It wasn't until 1500 that western civilization recorded any contact with marsupials. In that year, the Spanish explorer, Vincente Pinzon, picked up a female opossum in newly discovered Brazil and presented her to the monarchs Ferdinand and Isabella. The king and queen placed their royal fingers in her pouch and marveled at this unusual device for carrying the young.

The gestation period for an opossum is slightly less than thirteen days. At birth, the young are smaller than an inch, about the size of a bumblebee. Whereas the average adult opossum weighs between eight and thirteen pounds, fifteen newborn weigh less than an ounce. Female opossums can give birth to as many as twenty newborn young. Their hind limbs resemble embryonic buds and their forelimbs are muscular with well-developed claws. These forelimbs enable the underdeveloped opossum to accomplish the minor miracle of crawling several inches to the mother's pouch to find and attach to one of her nipples. It is important to note that there are only thirteen nipples available for nursing inside the pouch. This inevitably becomes a serious matter for the survival of smaller and weaker young who are members of litters larger than thirteen.

The young remain attached to the nipples until their eyes open, which occurs in approximately two months. At this time, they become ready to leave the pouch for short periods, often climbing on their mother's back or hanging from her sides. These outings serve to increase muscle strength and agility. Outside the pouch, the young can practice the use of their prehensile tails for grabbing and hanging onto surfaces. The young remain with the mother for another two months until they can maintain themselves. During this time, a second brood may develop such that a mother might be seen accompanied by two separate broods of considerably different size.

Among this marsupial's most unique traits is its ability to "play possum" when provoked or attacked. If chased by another animal, the opossum drops to the ground, drawing back its gums to bare its fifty teeth, more than any other North American mammal. It enters a catatonic stupor complete with slowed respirations. Predators determined to catch and consume an opossum are caught unaware by this behavior and eventually lose interest.

Ninety million years ago, relatives of the opossum shared the planet with dinosaurs. For the past sixty-five million years, opossums have remained structurally unchanged, surviving the Cretaceous-Paleogene extinction event when the giant meteor killed the dinosaurs. A couple factors have contributed to their success. First, the opossum is an omnivore. It will eat practically anything edible, including fruits, berries, leaves, grasses, insects, birds, small mammals, amphibians, and reptiles. Remarkably, they are immune to the venom of pit vipers, including rattlesnakes, copperheads, and cottonmouths. Second, the reproductive capabilities of the opossum are impressive. A female can have three litters in a single year. While many other animals have gone extinct, the opossum has extended its range to the north and west. Before 1900, there were no opossums in New England where they are now common. The opossum is a slow but steady swimmer, giving rise to the theory that opossums may have swum across the Cape Cod canal.

The opossum's interesting physical appearance has long been the subject of many folktales. One of these tales, told by the Cherokee, focuses on the opossum's hairless tail.

> *Long ago there was an opossum who constantly boasted to others about his wonderful, soft, bushy tail. When not boasting, the opossum was combing it throughout the day, every day. A rabbit, whose tail was just a bit of fluff, was annoyed at the constant attention the opossum solicited for his long, luxurious tail. Filled with jealousy, the rabbit decided to play a trick on the opossum and hired a barber to help him carry out his plan. The barber, a cricket, went with the rabbit to meet the opossum. Rabbit told the opossum that the cricket could make his tail even more beautiful, and the opossum was overjoyed. Imagining how attractive he would be at an upcoming*

gathering, he paid little attention to what the cricket was doing behind him.

When the opossum arrived at the gathering, he immediately began to brag about his soft, bushy tail. Instead of complimenting him, the animals began to laugh and point. Looking down at his tail, he couldn't believe what he saw. His wondrous hair was gone. His tail was pink and bare. The opossum was so embarrassed that he rolled over and played dead.

The evolution of opossums is fascinating to contemplate. The young opossums we cared for at the museum are part of an ancient lineage begun some ninety million years ago. Gazing at the tiny orphan opossums, I felt a connection to the past. Knowing that opossums have endured for millions of years, I felt hopeful that they too would survive.

Wishes on the Wind

Some of my earliest childhood memories are interwoven with the life cycle of dandelions. At age three, I picked a fist full of bright yellow dandelions, walked through my backyard and thrust them at my girlfriend who lived behind us. I don't exactly remember her reaction, nor why I was motivated to do it. What I can say is that dandelions are easy pickings for young children in spring. When you think about it, adult intervention is minimal. This is not a plant that adults protect from little hands. Any child can wander in their lawn picking to their hearts content. Not so with flowers growing in the garden or gracing the back deck. Flowers found in these locations are untouchables. A dandelion, on the other hand, is fair game and in the bargain focuses a child's attention on the flower head and what might be taking place there.

I am not sure when I first became aware that the white fluffballs which appeared a week later were the same plants. What mattered to me, as a child, was that these could be picked, and I could make the fluff fly. My friends and I would blow on the downy fluff, sending it skyward in directions and heights we hadn't imagined. Catching the fluffy parachutes once in flight was nearly impossible, even though we credited ourselves as being fast. Eventually we would get tired and one of us, with the intent to change the game, would flop on the ground, snapping off an almost perfect fluffball. All one had to do, he said, was take in a really deep breath, hold the fluffball in front of your lips and blow all the fluff off with one breath to make a wish come true. Sounded easy, so we gave it a go, finding out that clearing the head of even one fluffball was harder than we thought.

In my early childhood, dandelions were an introduction to what might be waiting for me in the world outdoors. These commonplace flowers, which grew with rich abundance, led me to make more random discoveries in nearby trees, bushes, tall grasses and even the forbidden gardens. At some point, I became aware that the yellow dandelion flowers in my yard had become the very same fluffballs we wished upon. It wasn't until later in life that I had the patience to return day after day to observe the changes required to get from flower to fluff.

Some educators would say that my focus on play makes sense in terms of the cognitive development of the young child. This educator finds that combining the opportunity to explore outdoors with imaginative play creates a joyful awareness that yearns to grow. Seen in this context, dandelions are companions in the education of young children rather than disasters in an otherwise perfect lawn.

As a young adult taking a college course in botany, I became interested in edible and medicinal plants. One evening while reading, I met up with my old friend, the dandelion. It seemed that every part of this plant had nutritional and medicinal value. A coffee substitute can be made from the roots. Its tender young leaves can be a tasty and nutritious addition to a salad, providing protein, iron, calcium, and vitamins A and C. Dandelion wine is made from the flowers. Unlike other invasive species that arrived in the New World by accident, dandelions were brought here on purpose, by European settlers who valued these nutritious plants.

These days I find it rewarding to spend time observing dandelions in early spring. In addition to their value as a food source for the human population, they serve a similar purpose for the many pollinators in search of nectar. Early spring days are a challenging time for insects. Opportunities for nectar gathering are determined by the availability of flowering plants. By late May, more of these native plants will have matured. Meanwhile, in early spring, flowers like the dandelion present the best chance to acquire nectar. When ingesting nectar, the insect drags its body over the flower picking up sticky grains of pollen. Leaving one flower to visit the next, the insect's process of feeding and transferring pollen eventually leads to the pollination of plants.

Dandelions thrive in inhospitable environments. Finding a dandelion that has burst through cracks in sidewalks or made its home on a rock pile never ceases to amaze me. Its success can be attributed to the myriad adaptations found in the structure of the plant. The rooting system consists of a thick deep taproot, accompanied by smaller, thinner roots which extend out from the sides. The taproot firmly holds the plant in place and secures the needed moisture and nutrients. It may come as a surprise to those who want to rid themselves of dandelions, but it doesn't help to pick only the flowers and leaves, or even dig out a portion of the root. You must dig out the entire plant to get the desired result. Dandelions can produce new growth even when the tap root has been broken into pieces. Even if chopped by the farmer's plow, each root section can grow a new dandelion.

The leaves form a ring at the base of the plant, spreading out in all directions, and keeping competitors at bay. Deeply serrated or toothed, the edges maximize photosynthesis. This leaf structure also explains the origin of its name, a corruption of the French description "dents de lion," meaning teeth of the lion.

Dandelions belong to the Asteraceae family, known for flower heads composed of numerous tiny flowers. The flower heads of dandelions are made up of individual strap-like ray flowers while others in its family have both ray and disc or tube-shaped flowers. Every day, the flowers open and close, usually opening in the early morning and closing shortly after noon, giving them the nickname "fairy clocks." The closing protects the male and female parts when the bees and other pollinators are finished with their morning rounds. On cloudy or rainy days, the flowers prefer to remain closed.

The seeds, perfectly designed to be carried by the wind, are sent into the sky by thermals of heated air rising from the sun-warmed grass. Each seed is attached to tiny white tufts called "pappus." Resembling the hairs in a white beard, the word is derived from the Greek word for grandfather. Like tiny parachutes, they rely on air resistance to keep them aloft. Upon landing, their arrow shaped seeds work their way into the soil aided by tiny barbs along the edges.

Throughout the ages, dandelions have appeared in folklore. They are considered omens of good luck, and even symbols of fertility. Some say you can send your loved one a message by blowing the seeds to him or her. Others believe that dandelions can help you tell the time of day.

It has been a long time since I wished upon a dandelion. Given what I know now and valuing their importance in stirring the native senses of young children, it might be time to make a new wish. My wish would be that we all could come to know and appreciate the plant for its many benefits. Greater awareness and better understanding of the interrelationships that make this world possible just might lead us to put down the noxious weed killer. That would mean less chemical run off into streams or vapors rising into the air. It could also serve to attract and sustain a wider variety of pollinators to yards and gardens.

The Resolute Snapper

Every year in May and early June, one of my students, a parent or a fellow teacher stops me in the hallway with rapid-fire questions about a snapping turtle they found in their yard. It's big, they tell me, with tiny eyes and big sharp claws and a long rubber-like tail with horny scales. "What do I do Mr. Newberger? Is my dog in danger? Do I have to stay inside? Should I call animal control? Will you come see it and, maybe, take it away?" At once I am struck with a multitude of feelings. As a teacher, I want to use this as a teachable moment no matter the age of my student. And I am pleased they had the opportunity to observe this impressive animal.

Snapping turtles have withstood the test of time, even surviving the effects of the meteor that led to the extinction of the dinosaurs. They remind us of an era when reptiles ruled the earth. Unlike the dinosaurs, the secret to the snapping turtle's success lies in its ability to adapt to a variety of conditions. Although it prefers swimming in shallow freshwater ponds, it is perfectly happy in the moving water of creeks or streams and even in brackish water in saltmarshes. Lying along the bottom or floating just above the surface, its dome-like shell is often covered with mud or algae.

While there is no need for alarm, one should be cautious around snapping turtles found on land as these females are focused on a very important task at hand: finding a suitable place to lay their eggs. Today's world features housing developments, shopping centers and roadways absent during the turtle's initial appearance on Earth. Streams, creeks, and small ponds adjacent to these developments will determine the watery habitats available for the female's choice of nesting spot. This has led to some startling discoveries by homeowners, bicyclists, and drivers.

More than once while driving, I've come to a complete stop, joining lines of traffic in both directions waiting for a snapping turtle to cross the road. It is recommended practice to do what you can on a highway to let a snapper make its own way. However, when I have found one to be in danger of being crushed under the wheel of an unsuspecting driver, I have pulled to the side of the road to figure out what assistance I might give. My general practice is to enlist another driver to stop any oncoming traffic, goad the turtle onto a car mat and pull her off the road making sure she is headed in the same direction as before. Some will tell you that if that doesn't work, there is a near perfect handle at the base of the shell where you can lift the turtle. However, you must be careful. The snapper is equipped with a big head, powerful jaws, and a razor-sharp beak that can strike with speed in any direction, although, in most cases, it will avoid a fight. Left alone it will go about its business, completely oblivious to human spectators. When encountering snapping turtles in the creek, they retreat into their shells and slowly swim away. Despite its vicious reputation, there are few stories of people being attacked by snappers.

Warmer spring days set the stage for the female snapping turtle to leave the water in search of the right spot to lay her eggs. It is surprising how far she will travel. It could be a mile or more away from the water. Digging a funnel shaped hole with her back legs, she quickly deposits the eggs, less than a minute apart. Initially they are quite soft, then soon they become hard and leathery, resembling small ping-pong balls. She will cover her eggs, leaving them to hatch in the warmth of the sun. As with many species, predation significantly affects the number of eggs left to hatch. Predators, including raccoons and skunks, eagerly add snapper eggs to their menu. To date, snapping turtles remain such prolific egg layers that many eggs can survive predation to hatch in eighty to ninety days.

Newly hatched baby turtles, about an inch in diameter, grow quickly. Like most reptiles, they must support themselves, without receiving food or guidance from their parents. Instinctively, they make their way to the nearest body of water. If interfered with and moved off course, they will eventually resume their original direction. Informed by their innate sense of gravity, they proceed downhill toward the water, successfully reaching their destination.

Carnivorous when young, an adult snapper will supplement its animal diet with plants, including marsh grasses and cattails. It has been known to come ashore to capture a small bird or reptile, but it will always return to the water to eat. Less frequently, a snapper will seize a slow-moving duck by the legs and drag it underwater. It is usually the sick or poorly adapted waterfowl, slow enough to be caught by a turtle, that serve as prey. The quicker, healthier animals easily escape a snapper no matter how sly and secretive it may be.

As the body temperature of cold-blooded animals is dictated by the surrounding air and water, snapping turtles survive winter by digging deep into the mud and burying themselves beneath the frost line. They can sometimes be found in the underground runways of muskrats and even underneath a beaver lodge. During the winter months, their metabolic rate slows such that their heartbeat is barely perceptible. Similar to the hibernation of some warm-blooded animals, scientists call this process brumation.

When the water temperature climbs into the fifties, snapping turtles emerge from their subterranean existence. In May and June, the females climb out of the water once again in search of the perfect nesting site. These days it seems that snappers are doing their best to adapt to a variety of human-constructed obstacles. I know of a few turtles who have chosen to establish a series of nests on the berm of a highway and others who have selected a sand pit or mulch pile. Each of these locations provides the opportunity for temperature control although could be rife with hazards.

Snapping turtles have witnessed the rise and fall of the mighty dinosaurs and they've seen endless themes of scale, feather, and fur. They have witnessed an unusual new species come down from the trees, building cities and empires. Hopefully, this new species will learn to leave the snapper alone so it can continue moving through the corridors of time, one of the last survivors of a bygone age.

Masters of the Surface Film

I am sitting along the banks of a small tributary of the Wissahickon Creek in suburban Philadelphia. It is midafternoon and the temperature is exceptionally warm. Brilliant rays of mid-day sun sparkle in the water below.

It is the middle of May and the creek is teeming with life. Along the gravel bottom, a crayfish walks slowly, then suddenly jets backward, disappearing under a rock. A backswimmer hangs on the underside of the surface film. Schools of three inch long black-nosed dace zoom through the water at Olympic speed. Above and below the water, scores of critters swim, glide, and whirl in what appears to be utter chaos.

Water is an incredible substance. It never ceases to amaze me that the combination of two invisible gases, hydrogen and oxygen, produces the liquid of life. The tendency for water molecules to attract one another, called cohesion, causes a tight film to form at the surface. Countless organisms, living both above and below the water's surface, depend on this film for their survival.

It is hard for me to fully appreciate the magnitude of this elastic water veneer which separates the wet world from the dry. I do not feel the film or experience the surface tension when I stick my finger in the water. I cannot see it with my eyes. I can, however, witness a tiny diving beetle on the surface film, digging its way beneath it. Or observe a whirligig beetle spinning nonstop in a series of ever-widening circles, living simultaneously above and below the surface film. I can watch a flying ant become trapped on the water's surface, never to fly again.

I first became aware of the surface film while watching water striders. Gently skating on top of the water or leaping from one spot to the next, the water strider swims, eats, mates, and dies in a world that unites air and water. Worldwide, there are 1700 identified species. Although they resemble spiders, they are insects and members of the Gerridae family. Some species are capable of flying, though they seldom take to the air unless forced to fly by an approaching predator. Others are strong divers that can carry bubbles of air underwater for long periods of time, returning to skate on top of the water. Like all insects, water striders have three pairs of legs. Their front legs are much smaller and allow the water strider to quickly grab its prey. The middle legs act as paddles and the back legs provide additional power, enabling the water strider to steer and brake.

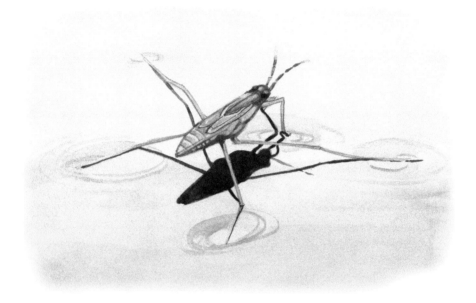

Their legs are covered with thousands of water-repellent microscopic hairs which trap air, increase water resistance, and provide buoyancy. I have never seen a water strider that looked wet. Each insect can support fifteen times its weight without sinking. Even in a torrential rainstorm, it stays afloat. Powerful legs enable the water striders to swim at speeds of one hundred body lengths per second, comparable to a six-foot tall person swimming 400 miles in an hour.

A mosquito larva, wriggling near the surface, becomes easy prey for nearby water striders. By way of tiny sensory organs on their legs, water striders detect faint vibrations in the water that lead them to their prey. Once a prey item is caught, the water strider inserts its sharp beak into the victim, filling it with digestive juices, dissolving the internal body organs. Once completely dissolved, the water strider drinks the liquefied inner organs of their prey, casting away the outer shells.

The antennae rest on the surface of the water, deciphering subtle movements in the ripples and waves. Some of these movements might lead a water strider to a good meal or serve to prevent a head-on collision with others. In early spring, a male will shake the surface of the water with his legs, sending out a repel signal to let others know he is in the area. If a female does not return the repel signal, the male will then send out a courtship signal. They become a mated pair when the female lowers her abdomen upon approach. The male remains attached until the eggs have been laid. The female water strider will gently pierce the surface film and lay her eggs in long strands on aquatic plants that lie beneath the film. The nymphs that hatch from these eggs will be tiny replicas of their parents. As they grow, they continue to molt, trading their old skins for new ones until they become adult water striders.

I find it fascinating to watch a water strider glide into view. This tiny body, held mid-air by six long legs, does nothing less than stand on water. As it paddles with halting strokes, moving between the dark and sunlit areas of the stream bank, I feel great respect. For here is a creature that truly lives on the edge between water and air.

Return of the Living Fossil

I spent the morning studying ancient history. No, I wasn't on the internet, in a library, or at a university. I was on the beach, observing our oldest living fossils, the horseshoe crabs. Underneath a brilliant blue sky, buffeted by spring winds and surrounded by the sounds of raucous shorebirds, I watched what I never could have imagined. Horseshoe crabs were everywhere. Their tracks were everywhere. Their eggs were everywhere and wherever the eggs were, there were birds. Hundreds and hundreds of migrating shorebirds were probing the sand and gorging themselves on tiny blue-green eggs.

Settling onto a rock in the jetty, I watched as the larger females made their way out of the surf to crawl on the sand accompanied by a random male or two, or sometimes three, clinging to each other. I was captivated by these saltwater creatures who had crawled out of the bay to lay their eggs in the sand. What I later learned was how vital these days were to both the crabs and the migrating birds.

A horseshoe crab is not a true crab. It is in an order all by itself. No other creature has mouthparts attached to its legs, so that it can eat only when walking. No other animal grows a complete new set of lenses for its eyes when it sheds its shell. Nothing else has book gills below the second body part, or a long stiff telson for a tail, or molts by walking headfirst out of the front of its shell. The ancestors of horseshoe crabs, the sea scorpions, left the sea over time and evolved into land creatures with eight legs. The horseshoe crab is closely related to arachnids, namely spiders, scorpions, mites, and ticks, and it has little in common with the true crabs.

In May and June, when spring tides flood the beaches and the water temperature reaches fifty-five degrees, the horseshoe crabs make their way to the shore. When the females reach the shallows, they release a jelly-like ooze attracting the males. The first male to respond to a lone female swims up from behind, latching onto her shell with two thumb-like claspers on his front legs. Sometimes, a second male, also attracted, may attach himself to the shell of the first male. Occasionally, a female is seen floating in on the tide dragging several males behind her, each one attached to the next. The female, with her mate(s) attached, reaches the sand beach and searches for a place to lay her eggs. Three or four times, she may stop to carve out a depression in the sand where she deposits several hundred blue-green eggs at a time. Once she has finished, the male moves over the eggs to fertilize them.

Some of the eggs that survive predation by shorebirds are washed from their sand beds by the tides. Others remain moist and protected in the sand where they hatch, producing a thin transparent "crystal ball" through which a tiny horseshoe crab can be seen. In two to four weeks, a half-inch tailless horseshoe crab larvae emerges. Carried out on the high tides, they drift in shallow waters where they continue to molt and soon acquire a tail. The first three years of their lives are the most dangerous due to their diminutive size, lack of defensive adaptations, and heavy predation by birds and ocean animals including sea turtles. Those who reach adulthood have successfully navigated life to mature between the ages of nine and twelve and are ready to begin the annual ritual of coming ashore to lay and fertilize their eggs.

The importance of these eggs is monumental to both the survival of the horseshoe crabs and to the animals that depend on them. Laying millions of eggs ensures future generations of horseshoe crabs. On that late May day when I arrived at a New Jersey beach on the Delaware Bay, there were hundreds of migrating shorebirds probing the sand for eggs. Red knots and ruddy turnstones had flown in from as far away as the tip of South America, 6,600 miles, to stop along these bay shores for the feast that would sustain their lives. They depend on the horseshoe crab's eggs to replenish weight lost on their journey north and to build energy stores for the coming reproductive season in the Arctic.

For 445 million years, relatives of horseshoe crabs have crawled out of the benthos onto the land to reproduce. That is a long time! With few modifications the horseshoe crab has survived the shifting location of the continents, the changing contours of the oceans, and the evolution and extinction of numerous creatures. Fossils from the earliest horseshoe crabs are found in strata from the Ordovician period before there was life on land.

There are several unique features that have assured the horseshoe crab's survival. As it is protected by an armored shell, most aquatic predators choose to leave the adults alone. Its anti-pathogen blood protects it from bacteria and other toxins present in the water. When the book gills are wet, it can breathe out of water for long periods of time. Additionally, a female horseshoe crab can produce up to 90,000 fertile eggs a year.

Over the past two decades, during my annual return visits, there was a decline in the numbers of both horseshoe crabs and birds, which concerned me. At first I thought they had chosen different beaches or that I was arriving too late or too early for that particular year. It turns out that I was not the only one alarmed. Many studies were in progress to identify reasons for the decline of the horseshoe crab population. Water pollution, habitat destruction, overfishing and even harvesting by the biomedical industry have impacted their survival. Each of these limiting factors are human created. Building along and next to beaches removes the natural sand slopes, often replacing them with impervious surfaces like concrete block which can trap crabs. Shipping lanes with deliveries to larger ports along the Delaware River and even smaller docking areas in the bay release fuel oils and other substances into the water. Formerly used as chicken feed and fertilizer in the 1900s, today's horseshoe crabs are now caught to use as bait for commercial eel and whelk fisheries.

In light of their rapid decline, many states have taken action to correct and improve some of these factors. Organizations and volunteers have dedicated countless hours to collecting data and working in a variety of ways to support their well-being. As one would expect, with the decline in breeding horseshoe crab populations, came the devastation of the migratory bird population. There is hope that it is not too late to turn the tide. As the number of horseshoe crabs increases, an increase in the numbers of migrating birds will follow.

The horseshoe crab has contributed to some major breakthroughs in medical science. In 1956, Fred Bang at the Marine Biological Laboratory in Chicago found that the copper-based blood of horseshoe crabs could play a significant role in detecting bacterial toxins or endotoxins. Amoebocytes, a component of their blood, were discovered and developed into a clotting agent known as Limulus Amoebocyte Lysate (LAL). This agent, occurring solely in the blood of horseshoe crabs, is used to test medical devices, drugs, and vaccines for the presence of endotoxins. Since that time, pharmaceutical laboratories have harvested and bled live horseshoe crabs, releasing them once the process is completed. One synthetic alternative was developed in China in the late 1990s, however it has not been given FDA approval. Currently with the advent of the Covid pandemic and the resulting vaccine development by a host of pharmaceutical companies, additional research is being done to find an alternative to LAL. Given the decline in the numbers of crabs, relieving them from the pressure of their donations could only result in supporting their populations.

When two seemingly unrelated events coincide in an unlikely and meaningful fashion, it is called synchronicity. There is no better example than the rendezvous of horseshoe crabs and shorebirds, uniting continents and clearly illustrating that we live on one planet where everything is interconnected. Long before the 1968 Apollo mission took its iconic picture of earth from outer space, showing us a beautiful blue-green planet with no divisions of countries or states, the shorebirds and horseshoe crabs demonstrated that we live on one planet, and we are all interdependent.

Plants with a Taste for Little Beasts

Life is more complex than we have been led to believe. Years ago, during a college field trip to a quaking bog, I found a steadfast tenet of my education in tatters. Like most students, I learned that plants produce the energy they need through photosynthesis and animals hunt, trap or gather food. Yet here was an exception. I was looking at plants that have a taste for little beasts.

Green plants convert sunlight, water, and carbon dioxide into simple sugars. This process, called photosynthesis, forms the basis of the food chain which moves energy from the sun to plants and on to animals, making life on this planet possible. To sustain growth and remain vigorous, minerals found in the soil, nitrogen, phosphorus, potassium, and calcium, are absorbed by the roots of plants. Carnivorous plants prosper in nutrient-poor soils, where they have little competition from other plant species.

Far from science fiction, animal-trapping plants are not mere fantasies from the pens of imaginative writers. Despite astonishing legends of man-eating shrubs, tiny frogs are the largest prey captured by carnivorous flora. Most food items are insects and small crustaceans. Fortunately, we can find some of them in the northeastern United States. Sundews, pitcher plants, and bladderworts, each with their own adaptations for attracting and devouring prey, dominate bogs in the northeast.

The sundew doesn't actively pursue its prey. Like flypaper, it remains motionless relying on the reddish hairs covering its leaves to do the work. Glands found at the tip of each thin reddish hair produce a powerful

adhesive, digestive enzymes, and sweet-smelling secretions. Lured by its secretions, or simply seeking a landing platform, an ill-fated insect that alights on the leaf of a sundew will find itself stuck fast. Over time, the tiny hairs will bend around the trapped insect and smother it. Once immobilized, the nutrients from the insect's body will be available for absorption.

Shiny red pinwheel-shaped flowers call attention to the pitcher plant; however, the leaves do the work. They form a close-fitting vase which acts as a water reservoir to imprison insects and other small animals. Attracted to nectar and bright patterns near the top of the opening, the victim enters by foot or wing. Led by the downward pointing bristles on the leaves, the unfortunate intruder descends to the center of the vase. The slippery walls of the plant make escape nearly impossible. Repeated attempts to fly or crawl out only end in exhaustion. Before long, the victim drowns in the liquid at the bottom of the pitcher plant, soon to be assimilated by digestive enzymes therein.

Both the sundew with its flypaper trap and the pitcher plant with its pitfall trap evolved passive methods for capturing prey. By contrast,

the bladderwort actively ensnares its victims. These delicate looking plants can be found floating on still water. The bladders which adorn the submerged filament-like leaves serve a dual purpose. During spring and summer, the bladders act like floats, allowing the yellow or purple flowers to rise above the water surface for pollination. Each submerged bladder contains a trap door surrounded by tiny plant hairs. When an animal grazes along the surface of these tiny threadlike bristles, it encounters trigger hairs. Instantly, the trap is sprung, and water is sucked inside the bladder, dragging the animal along. Once caught, the trap door closes to prevent escape. Most of its victims are water fleas, copepods, and other small crustaceans, although tiny fish and tadpoles occasionally get their heads caught in the bladders. Bladderwort is known for possessing the fastest trapping mechanism found in nature. The entire process takes only a fraction of a second.

One of the best places to see carnivorous plants is in a bog where they have carved out an unusual niche for themselves amongst some of the more primitive plant forms, the mosses and ferns. Created over time by accumulating plant debris, a bog's floating mat of sphagnum moss, or peat, is replenished only by rainfall. Minimal drainage, high acidity, and poorly aerated water distinguishes bogs from other wetlands. By contrast, swamps are covered with trees while marshes are filled with grasses, sedges, and rushes. Home to specific tree species of spruce, fir, and tamarack, bogs are most often associated with the north country, although they can be found further south in locations with little drainage.

I have visited bogs from the Great Okefenokee Swamp in Georgia to coastal Maine. Unexpectedly, I've discovered miniature bogs in the rain-drenched swales of the Cape Cod sand dunes. Bogs draw me in like a magnet. Over the years it has brought me great joy to head out with a group of campers and colleagues to explore a unique bog community. Our excitement is tempered by the fact that this is a fragile place with its slow growing and sensitive plants. It requires cautious footfalls and thoughtful interactions.

The extraordinary beauty of these peculiar plants has captured the imagination of scientists and laymen for centuries. Charles Darwin devoted a book to observations and experiments he conducted with insectivorous plants. Unfortunately, these plants are threatened when wetlands are drained or filled. To the untrained eye, a waterlogged bog appears unproductive and worthless. Closer observation reveals untold treasures. Bogs are fascinating and priceless habitats worthy of preservation.

I Brake for Wildflowers

"What is a weed? A plant whose virtues have not yet been discovered."
–Ralph Waldo Emerson

I waited patiently through the February snows and the March winds to welcome the return of spring wildflowers. I visited fields of wildflower remnants, withered and brown, that harbored seed pod promises. I paged through books in anticipation of the form and colors they would lend to the landscape. Then, at last, they were here!

The numbers of wildflowers slowly increase as the season progresses. May and June seem especially prolific when the sun spends up to fourteen hours above the horizon. Numerous red, orange, blue, and yellow flowers open to face the sun. It is the photoperiod, or day-length timetable of each plant, together with warming temperatures and adequate precipitation that signals them to bloom. Most wildflowers are perennials returning year after year while some are biennials with a two-year lifespan. Each returns to bloom during the same time every year, assuring us of fields and meadows vibrant with color for months to come.

To what end is this array of color and form? Wildflowers have little concern for pleasing the eye of the human beholder. Their goal is to attract pollinators. Pollinators are key to the survival of most plants. They are equipped with the necessary tools to distribute pollen found on the anthers (male parts) of one flower to the pistil (female part) of another. A potential pollinating insect must be lured to a flower either through sight or smell. Upon landing, the pollen it carries from another plant of the same species must rub off its body to impregnate the pistil, or female part, usually found in the flower's center. Seeking a nectar meal, its long tongue, or proboscis, probes for nectar while its belly or back curves at just the right angle to pick up or deposit pollen. During this process, the insect acquires pollen and moves off to repeat the process with another flower.

Queen Anne's lace and boneset are examples of perennial wildflowers whose nectar can be found as a flat shiny layer at the base of their pistils. This placement of nectar, so fully exposed, is perfect for insects with short proboscides, including flies, wasps, and ants.

The nectar of meadowsweet and chickweed is partially hidden. Flies and bees with medium-sized proboscides as well as several species of butterflies visit these flowers. These plants produce large quantities of pollen; however, the nectar can only be seen in bright sunlight.

Butterflies, moths, and bees with long proboscides visit orchids, lilies, legumes, and mints. Their proboscides are well adapted to withdraw nectar concealed below the pistil. Bright colors are a lure to day-flying insects and indicators on the petals such as streaks, hairs, and dots often guide them to the nectar. Red is preferred by butterflies, yellow and white by moths, and blue and violet by bees.

A few plants, like our wild roses, Canada mayflower, and spiderwort, are without nectar and therefore not attractive to butterflies, moths, and wasps. These plants make up for their lack of nectar by producing copious amounts of pollen. Their visitors include honeybees, who fill their pollen baskets, returning to the hive where it is used as larval food.

Surprisingly, there are many plants that are pollinated by beetles, including magnolias, spicebush and goldenrod. They are specifically focused on gathering pollen rather than nectar for the nutrients pollen offers them. One hundred fifty million years ago, they were pollinating cycads, ancient seed plants which resemble today's palm trees. It wasn't until fifty million years later that bees appeared.

Plants in the Asteraceae family attract a wide range of insects. These flowers are composed of many tiny florets growing on a densely packed head, arranged like spokes on a wheel or in aggregates of tube-like disks. Daisies, coneflowers, asters, and goldenrods are conspicuous examples. Many plants in the Asteraceae family came from Europe and Asia in the ballast of ships. They tend to grow along roadsides and other disturbed areas, where there is little competition from our native vegetation. Nectar found in these plants provides food for a variety of insects that haven't specialized on a particular food source.

Old Noah Webster defined a weed as "a plant out of place." Granted, in terms of human goals and objectives, a wildflower may be "out of place," but never in nature's grand scheme. Wildflowers are key determinants for the survival of all pollinators.

Every month, from April through October, I join a group of plant enthusiasts who look for wildflowers at local parks and nature preserves. Observing wildflowers helps us learn habitat requirements, limiting factors, and ways our lives connect with the plant kingdom. We meet again in February, after the flowers have gone to seed, to better our identification skills and to examine seed pods and desiccated floral structures. While this is an interest of mine and my enthusiastic friends, it is an interest that is spreading like the wildflowers themselves. Case in point, I was passed on the road by a car with a bumper sticker which read "I Brake for Wildflowers."

Up From the Underground

The night was alive with the sounds of frogs. It had been raining for the last twelve hours and, from my human perspective, I imagined hundreds of frogs having the time of their lives.

Unlike the frogs, I wasn't enjoying the rain. I had rented a dune shack on the Provincelands of Cape Cod and wanted to be out exploring the dunes and beach. Instead, all explorations had been postponed and I was spending the evening reading indoors. Frustrated, I tried going to bed early, thinking I would be able to get a head start in the morning. Impossible. Rain thundered on the rooftop.

Every bog, hollow, and swale around the shack resounded with the calls of green frogs, bullfrogs, and Fowler's toads. Shortly before midnight, I noticed a very different sound. There was a series of raucous squawks, resembling the caw of crows. While I was familiar with most of the amphibian sounds on Cape Cod, this was something new. I had to investigate. I put on my raincoat and rain pants, picked up my five-battery flashlight, and headed off in the direction of the sound. To put it mildly, I've been out under more pleasant conditions. Pelted by sheets of rain and hounded by swarms of mosquitoes, my curiosity kept me going.

It wasn't long before I heard a low grunting noise under my feet. I stopped to shine my flashlight, checking for any sign of animal life. Seeing none, I kept walking until I came to a series of temporary pools nestled in a wild cranberry bog. Here the sound swelled from a muffled groan to a loud, almost deafening roar. Turning my flashlight on, I found that everywhere I looked there were small, wrinkled bodies with big bulging eyes. I was standing in a gathering, known as a congress, of eastern spadefoot toads.

I had read about eastern spadefoots and found descriptions of their characteristics and behaviors intriguing. Listed as threatened under the Massachusetts Endangered Species Act, they have rarely been seen with only thirty-two locations recorded since 1982. Eastern spadefoots live most of their lives deep underground. It is the siren call of a dark and stormy night that brings them to the surface to breed. They appear for a matter of hours and then disappear for days, weeks, or perhaps years.

I bent down and gently picked one up to examine it closely. Its body reminded me of a prune. Around the head, the skin seemed smooth, wrinkling at every turn along the rest of its body. Its two back feet were each equipped with a long sickle-shaped toe resembling a "spade" used for digging.

It was the eyes, though, that captivated me. Spaced far apart, they appeared to pop out of its head. Gleaming at me on this dark rainy night, the eyes seemed to speak of another age when amphibians first crawled out of the water and onto the land. Remembering that the spadefoot belongs to a primitive family predating any other living amphibian, I felt like I was staring eye-to-eye into a time long past.

When I placed the animal back in the water it quickly hopped onto another toad. There wasn't any time to lose. Warm torrential rains are infrequent and once they end, the toads return underground. This night was for breeding, and survival of the species demands sole dedication to this one purpose.

Adjacent to the silent breeding pairs, I watched single males emitting loud plaintive cries. When these males called, their throat sacs swelled to a size larger than their heads, serving as resonators that carried their calls over great distances. Listening to them on this night, I would describe their sound as a low ear-piercing moan that sends shivers up the spine.

Drenched and exhilarated, I returned to the dry comfort of the dune shack. In the morning, when I went back to check on them, most of the toads had disappeared. Only a few stragglers remained on site. Still, evidence of a busy night could be seen along the stems of plants, where there were now long irregular bands of eggs encased in a jelly-like ooze in single and double rows. Since then, I have read that each female can lay 2500 eggs. Remarkable.

Two days later, I returned to the same site and not a single spadefoot toad could be found. Checking the pool of water, I saw many black, tiny creatures swimming in all directions. I leaned over and scooped one up to find that it was a tadpole approximately a quarter inch in size. The cranberry bog was teeming with the offspring of the toads.

In less than two weeks, the surviving tadpoles will transform themselves into tiny toadlets. They will use their well-equipped feet to tunnel into the soil quickly disappearing perhaps for a year or more. Nobody seems quite sure how deep they go, however a gravedigger once found a spadefoot toad three feet two inches below the surface. The head was bent downwards, and the feet were tucked underneath the body.

On any given warm and dark night, when the barometer drops, the rain comes pouring down, and the mosquitoes rule the skies, my thoughts race back to the dunes of the Provincelands. Could this the night? Have the spadefoots returned? Are they calling? I hope so. What a gift it was to witness something so extraordinary!

Appendix

Community Science - People, Nature and Science

by Ron Smith

In a time of great concern for the natural world, people everywhere are mobilizing to help. From wetland habitats to sandy beaches, to fields and meadows and even our urban landscapes, ordinary people are counting, monitoring, restoring, and documenting species and habitats of all kinds. The reality is that there simply are not enough scientists to cover all the conservation projects and sites that are needed to protect biodiversity. With a modest amount of training and coordination, school children and their teachers, nature clubs and people from all walks of life can participate in community science projects to aid scientists and organizations in their efforts to understand the conservation status of species and ecosystems. By coming together, we can educate others, restore habitats, and protect the organisms that provide essential ecosystem services and inspire wonder and excitement about the natural world.

Over the past twenty-five years, I have led community science projects and efforts which focus on amphibians, freshwater mussels, insects, shorebirds, and marine invertebrates. Below I offer a glimpse into our project on horseshoe crab conservation on the Delaware Bay shores. The passage gives perspective on the field experiences, collaboration and educational efforts that are key to a successful community science endeavor.

Fortescue, NJ on the Delaware Bay

I love early starts on the Delaware Bayshores. Driving with my windows down along NJ Avenue on the bayfront of the small community of Fortescue, NJ, the cool spring breeze sets the stage for a comfortable rescue. We parked the cars along the seawall of the fishing beach and gathered to review the protocol for the day. Gloves were distributed, notebooks and pencils provided, and we walked onto the beach. The winds that would keep the insects at bay had pushed the tide high overnight on the beach. A busy day was in store. With headlamps on, we scanned the narrow beach that would widen a bit more as the tide ebbed. The rounded carapace of thousands of horseshoe crabs at the water's edge and the scattering of overturned crabs higher up on the beach revealed the work ahead. We were here to rescue horseshoe crabs.

Since the mid 1990s, I had been bringing students to see the horseshoe crab spawn on the Delaware Bayshores. The largest spawning event of its kind in the world, the eggs deposited by these ancient invertebrates fuels the northbound migration of shorebirds returning from South America and heading to the Arctic to nest. Some of the very same birds that we count in the fall at North Brigantine are among the hundreds of thousands who arrive for the feeding frenzy in May. To visit one of these beaches—Fortescue, Moore's Beach, Money Island, or a dozen other sites—is to visit an ancient world. For hundreds of millions of years, long before the dinosaurs walked the earth, horseshoe crabs have been emerging from the coastal waters to reproduce. Largely unchanged over geologic time, the male uses his modified front walking legs to hook onto the female. She will dig down into the sand at high tide and deposit a few thousands eggs that he will then fertilize. Night spawns on the highest tides reveal peak activity, but I have seen impressive gatherings of crabs even in the daylight hours. The surplus of eggs that are dug up by other females or washed out by tide and wave are available as a calorie-rich food supply for the shorebirds. Among them, the red knots have arrived as little more than feather and bone having flown non-stop from Brazil in anticipation of the egg feast.

Some of my best lessons on Natural History, Evolution, Ecology and Conservation have occurred on the bayshores. It's hard to imagine a more engaging classroom. It was during one of these very lessons several years ago that a student asked a question that brought about the Horseshoe Crab Community Science Project. During our early years of Delaware Bay visits, we would come across stranded, overturned, or trapped horseshoe crabs and, knowing the importance of their survival to that of the shorebirds, we would always rescue them. On that busy day when our efforts went more to rescuing crabs than watching shorebirds feed, one of my students wondered aloud about just how many crabs were there to rescue? We looked down the beach, then at each other and the next natural thing to establish was ... well, let's count them! More important than the hundreds we would count that afternoon was the plan to begin a more systematic count the next spring season. We scheduled to visit Fortescue every Friday during the spawn to survey the same stretch of beach every visit.

One year later, we were turning in counts that could go as high as 1000 crabs on a one kilometer strand. A pile of concrete rubble had been placed along the beach to protect New Jersey Avenue from the erosive power of wave, storm, and tide, but it was a death sentence for any horseshoe crab that was washed into the debris. With a telson that could kickstand into the sand to right themselves when turned over, this approach was useless once trapped in the rubble. Our rescue numbers were turned in to the NJ Division of Fish and Wildlife and two things happened as a result. The urgency to plan for some sort of restoration at Fortescue was heightened and, as of the following season, a plan to organize a more expanded effort to rescue horseshoe crabs was put together by the state and several conservation groups on the bayshores. That first year the students in my classes were responsible for almost half of the horseshoe crabs rescued on the New Jersey side of the Delaware Bay. As of this past season, more than a hundred thousand horseshoe crabs were rescued by volunteers associated with the Return the Favor NJ project. My students have joined forces with scientists, community members, college students and many other volunteers and now about twenty beaches are surveyed daily during May and June in the spring.

These student volunteers have gone on to participate in horseshoe crab beach restoration, establish educational programs for elementary age students and present their findings at scientific conferences. I now have returning students each spring teach the new recruits the methods of rescue and I have had several students who continue to participate right through college and after graduation, often bringing their families to assist.

As a teenager, I recall the awesome spectacle of the horseshoe crab spawn. Visiting Seabreeze, NJ on fishing trips with my uncle back in 1986, I first learned of the connection between horseshoe crabs and migratory shorebirds. At the time, I had no idea that during those same spring visits, scientists were putting together some of the critical pieces to the conservation puzzle on the bayshores. Crab numbers would plummet in the years that would follow, and the shorebird numbers would follow, especially the red knots. In the mid 1990s when I brought my first groups of students to the bayshores, I was shocked by the changes that occurred in under a decade. Today I celebrate the actions and dedication of the volunteers who work tirelessly every spring to protect shorebirds and rescue horseshoe crabs.

It happens every rescue season that a visitor to the beach will stop me to ask what I am doing. It is worth my time to take a few minutes to share the wonder of this age-old ecological phenomenon and the recent effort to bring together students, educators, researchers, families, and volunteers to save the life of a creature connected to shorebirds, connected to the bay, and connected to our very health and well-being.

Learn more about horseshoe crabs and the horseshoe crab rescues at:

horseshoecrab.org/conservation
returnthefavornj.org
hscrabrecovery.org

Craig Newberger

Author Craig Newberger served as the Lower School science coordinator at Germantown Academy in Pennsylvania for over three decades. Combining hands-on investigations with outdoor explorations, Craig nurtured a passion for science and nature in thousands of inquisitive minds. He led a variety of natural science trips for his students and their families, ranging from Costa Rica to Cape Cod. Craig's belief in immersing students in firsthand experiences inspired him to dedicate decades of summers in Maine where he and his wife, Trudy, directed the National Audubon Society Youth Ecology Camp on Hog Island, founded and directed the Family Camp, and joined the instructional team for Audubon's camp for educators. Craig has also worked as a naturalist at the Cape Cod Museum of Natural History and directed an environmental education program connected with the Cape Cod National Seashore. Craig plays guitar and hammered dulcimer and he is known for his sing-a-longs at assemblies and campfires.

Steve Morello

Steve Morello is an award-winning photographer, writer, and storyteller, known for telling a story with his images. Steve created the Little River Photo Workshops to share his skill and craft with others on his property in North Berwick, Maine. Steve is a National Geographic certified photo instructor and teaches for National Geographic and Lindblad Expeditions on expeditions around the planet. He is the author of *The Traveling Nature Photographer*.

Sherrie York

A self-taught printmaker and compulsive wanderer of landscapes, Sherrie York finds her inspiration in the natural world. A long-ago college field trip to draw backyard chickens was the genesis of a career that has encompassed environmental education, natural history illustration, and fine art. Her illustration clients have included several national and international conservation organizations and her fine art is included in corporate, private, and museum collections worldwide.

Ron Smith

Ron Smith established the environmental science and education program in the Haddonfield School district where he currently teaches. With faculty and staff from the Academy of Natural Sciences of Drexel University, Ron leads community science projects along the coast of New Jersey with a focus on shorebirds and horseshoe crabs. He directs the Drexel University Environmental Science Leadership Academy and founded the Life Science Field Training Institute for Pinelands Preservation Alliance, a program that trains educators in field methods in community science.

Acknowledgments

It has always been a goal of mine to share with others the fascination I feel about the natural world. As a teacher, program director or naturalist, I have spent most of my life offering hands-on experiences that generate curiosity. In writing this series of essays, images of friends, family, teachers, and students surfaced to accompany me in the process. These memories and their impact have come alive in *Spring Processional*. Whether we searched for spring's first flowers, looked for woodcocks in the fields, or listened to the chorus of spring peepers, my life has been enriched by all that we've shared. Thank you.

Most importantly, I need to thank Trudy Phillips, my wife, best friend, and soul mate. Trudy and I worked closely together to edit and fine-tune the writing of this book. An award-winning educator, Trudy was the Director for Environmental Education at the Perkiomen Watershed Conservancy for twenty-six years. I also wish to thank our daughter Heather, fashion stylist and author, for sharing her expertise and inspiration.

My mother, Gloria Newberger, is responsible for instilling the values I have today. Currently in her nineties and living in Florida, she enjoys outside walks every day. As a dedicated advocate for learning, my mother championed my curiosity and appreciation for beauty. My mother and my kind and supportive sister, Nancy, read my writing as it developed and offered valuable feedback.

I wish to thank Scott Weidensaul, Ted Gilman, Heidi Rader, and Tom Tyning for carefully reading my manuscript and offering invaluable feedback.

Finally, I am indebted to Ed Flickinger, publisher of Grackle Books, for taking on this project. I am deeply appreciative of his advice and expertise.